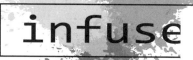

Acts
church on the edge
PART ONE

by Cathie Brasser
and Micki Hilbrand

FAITH
ALIVE®
Christian Resources

Grand Rapids, Michigan

"You will be my witnesses . . .
to the ends of the earth."
—Acts 1:8

We are grateful for the many comments and helpful suggestions of interested small groups and leaders who contributed to the development of this study.

In this study of Acts the lessons are written by Cathie Brasser, and the Break Away (at-home readings) are written by Micki Hilbrand.

Cover photo: shutterstock

Maps: Matthew P. Faber

Printed in the United States of America.

We welcome your comments. Call us at 1-800-333-8300 or email us at editors@faithaliveresources.org.

ISBN 978-1-59255-527-7

5 4 3 2 1

Contents

The World of the Early Church (First Century A.D.)

CORSICA

ITALY

ADRIATIC SEA

DALMATIA

MACEDON

●Rome

Three Taverns● ●Forum of Appius

●Puteoli

SARDINIA

EPIRUS

TYRRHENIAN SEA

IONIAN SEA

●Rhegium

SICILY

Syracuse ●

Malta

NORTH AFRICA

Cyre

LIB

N

200 ┤ mi

200 ┤ km

MOESIA

BLACK SEA

THRACE

PONTUS

essalonica
Philippi
Neapolis
Amphipolis
Apollonia
Samothrace

BITHYNIA

GALATIA

Berea

Mt. Olympus

AEGEAN
SEA

Troas
Assos

MYSIA

Mitylene

Pergamum

ASIA

CAPPADOCIA

Thyatira

Kios

Sardis

Philadelphia

Pisidian
Antioch

LYCAONIA

Delphi

orinth

Smyrna

LYDIA

PHRYGIA

Iconium

Athens

Samos

Ephesus
Laodicea

PISIDIA

Lystra

Cenchrea

Patmos

Miletus

Colosse

Derbe

CHAIA

CILICIA

parta

Cos

Cnidus

Attalia

PAMPHYLIA

Tarsus

Perga

Issus

RHODES

Patara

LYCIA

Myra

Antioch

Seleucia

Phoenix

CRETE

Salmone

CYPRUS

Salamis

SYRIA

Fair Havens

Lasea

Paphos

THE GREAT SEA
(MEDITERRANEAN SEA)

PHOENICIA

Sidon

Tyre

Damascus

Ptolemais

SAMARIA

Caesarea

Jordan R.

JUDEA

Jerusalem

Salt Sea

Alexandria

EGYPT

Nile R. Delta

ARABIA

5

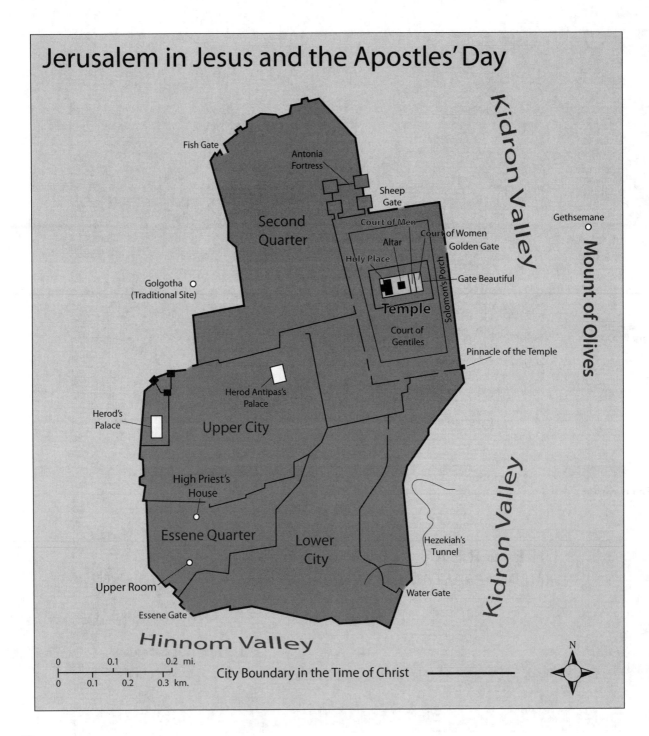

Jerusalem in Jesus and the Apostles' Day

Fish Gate

Antonia Fortress

Sheep Gate

Second Quarter

Court of Men

Court of Women

Altar

Golden Gate

Holy Place

Solomon's Porch

Gate Beautiful

Golgotha (Traditional Site)

Temple

Court of Gentiles

Pinnacle of the Temple

Herod Antipas's Palace

Herod's Palace

Upper City

High Priest's House

Hezekiah's Tunnel

Essene Quarter

Lower City

Upper Room

Water Gate

Essene Gate

Kidron Valley

Gethsemane

Mount of Olives

Kidron Valley

Hinnom Valley

| 0 | | 0.1 | | 0.2 mi. |
| 0 | 0.1 | 0.2 | 0.3 km. |

City Boundary in the Time of Christ

N

Glossary

Abraham—father of the Jewish people (Israel), renowned for his faith in God's promises (Gen. 12:1-7; 15:6; Heb. 11:8-16). Also called "the father of all who believe" in Christ (Rom. 4:11).

angels—supernatural beings created by God to be messengers, to carry out God's will in this world, and to serve and care for all who belong to God (Ps. 91:11-12).

apostle—"one sent forth"; refers to a messenger sent on a special mission. The New Testament apostles were leaders in the early Christian church; they were specially chosen by Jesus to be his witnesses (Mark 3:13-19; Luke 24:48; Acts 1:8, 21-25; 9:1-15; 1 Cor. 9:1-2).

baptism, baptize—the act of sprinkling with or immersion in water as a sign of God's claim on a person's life to be part of the covenant family of God. Baptism is an outward sign that Christ's blood washes the believer clean of the guilt of sin.

blasphemy—scoffing at or misusing the name of God.

Christ—see **Jesus Christ**, **Messiah**.

circumcision—removal of the male foreskin. God commanded Abraham and his descendants to do this as a sign that they belonged to God and as a symbol of the cutting away of sin from their lives (Gen. 17). In the New Testament circumcision is replaced with baptism in Christ. True circumcision is of the heart, not the flesh (Jer. 4:4; Col. 2:9-12).

covenant—a mutually binding agreement between two parties. In the Old Testament God made covenants with his chosen people Israel in which he promised to be their God, and they pledged to be faithful to him. These agreements form the basis of their relationship with God.

David—Israel's greatest king in the Old Testament. The Lord promised that one of David's descendants would rule faithfully on his throne forever (2 Sam. 7). As Matthew 1 shows, Jesus Christ is that "Son of David."

disciple—a follower; one who is taught. This term refers commonly to followers to Jesus.

faith—defined in Hebrews 11:1 as "being sure of what we hope for and certain of what we do not see." Can be defined in simple terms as "belief and trust." True saving faith is a gift that consists of knowledge and confidence—a sure knowledge by which we accept as true all that God has revealed in his Word, and confidence that all our sins are forgiven for Jesus' sake.

fast (fasting)—ancient religious practice in which people go without food and/or water for set periods; in the Jewish tradition fasting was often accompanied by prayer to God for help in a time of great need (see 2 Chron. 20:2-4).

the Father—the first person of the Trinity. The other two persons are God the Son (Jesus Christ) and God the Holy Spirit. They are three persons in one being.

flog—to beat with a rod or whip.

Gentiles—all people who are not Jews.

good news—see **gospel**.

gospel—literally means "good news" and refers to the message of God's salvation from sin and the promise of eternal life through Christ.

grace—God's undeserved favor and forgiving love. Jesus is the full expression of God's grace for the salvation of all who believe in him as Lord and Savior (Eph. 2:8-10).

holy—pure; set apart to bring glory to God.

Holy Spirit—the third person of the Trinity. The other two persons are God the Father and God the Son (Jesus Christ). They are three persons in one being. The Holy Spirit convicts us of sin, works true faith in our hearts, and empowers us to live holy lives. The Spirit's presence in our hearts guarantees that we will receive God's promises (John 16:7-15; Rom. 8:11; Eph. 1:13-14).

hope—in combination with faith this means looking ahead in solid trust to the fulfillment of all God's promises (Heb. 7:19; 11:1).

idols—anything worshiped or honored ahead of or in place of God. Idolatry can mean bowing down to a physical image of a god; it can also mean allowing one's possessions or desires to become more important than God.

Isaac—Abraham and Sarah's son, who inherited all the promises God made with Abraham.

Isaiah—a Hebrew prophet from around 700 B.C. who foretold the coming of Christ (Messiah) and described his service and suffering.

Jacob—Isaac's son whom God renamed Israel (Gen. 32:28) and who became the patriarch of the twelve tribes of Israel.

Jerusalem—Israel's historic capital city. As the location for God's temple, it became the center for the Jewish religion and the spiritual headquarters of the nation of Israel.

Jesus Christ—the sinless Son of God, who gave his life as the payment for our sin. *Jesus* means "Savior," and *Christ* means "Anointed One." He is the second person of the Trinity. The other two persons are God the Father and God the Holy Spirit. They are three persons in one being. See also **Messiah**.

Jews—the people of Israel, descendants of Abraham; God's special people chosen to be a blessing to all other nations (Gen. 12:2-3).

justified—declared forgiven and righteous by God through repentance and faith in Jesus Christ. Those who are justified are not merely pardoned: the demands of the law have been fully met through the atoning work of Christ.

kingdom of God—God's rule over all things, especially evident in the lives of his people, who follow Jesus and believe in him as Savior.

last days—generally considered to be the period ranging from the time of the Messiah's (Jesus') birth until his second coming (see Acts 2:17).

law—(the law of Moses) the Ten Commandments and hundreds of ceremonial and social laws given by God to the nation of Israel and prescribed in Genesis through Deuteronomy.

the Law and the Prophets—the teachings of the Old Testament. See **Scriptures**.

Levites—descendants of Jacob's son Levi. God set aside this tribe to be priests, to care for the house of God, to attend to the details of worship, and to teach the Israelites God's ways. They continued in this role until Jesus fulfilled all the requirements of the law and the ceremonial laws were no longer necessary (see Heb. 7-10).

lots (casting lots)—a method of decision making that involves throwing or choosing objects in order to know God's will. Lots approved by God for use in ancient Israel were the Urim and Thummim (Ex. 28:30).

Messiah—the promised deliverer of God's people. Both the Hebrew word *Messiah* and the Greek word *Christ* mean "Anointed One." Through the prophets God promised to send the Messiah, the Savior-King, to deliver his people from oppressors and to rule in righteousness forever. The people misunderstood those promises, however, and looked for a Messiah who would be a political ruler and gather an army to rout all physical enemies (see John 6:15; Acts 1:6). But as Jesus revealed through his work and teaching, the Messiah came to save God's people from the oppression of sin and death and to give them new life forever with God. He rules today in heaven at the right hand of the Father, and when he comes again at the end of time, he will fully establish God's everlasting kingdom of righteousness on earth. (See Matt. 26:63-64; John 16:5-16; 1 Cor. 15; Rev. 21:1-5; 22:1-5.)

Moses—the Old Testament prophet who led the Israelites out of slavery in Egypt and brought them to the promised land of Canaan. During his leadership Moses received from God and taught Israel the laws that would govern them as God's chosen people.

Nazareth—a small town in the province of Galilee where Jesus grew up.

Passover—This feast took place each spring to celebrate the Israelites' exodus from slavery in Egypt. The name commemorates God's protection of Israelite households during a final plague sent to convince the Egyptian king (pharaoh) to let the Israelites go. God promised that upon seeing the blood of a sacrificed lamb on the doorframes of a house, God would *pass over* that house and not allow the plague of death to take the life of the firstborn there (see Ex. 12). The feast pointed to our ultimate deliverance from sin through the sacrifice of Jesus Christ, the Lamb of God (John 1:29; 1 Cor. 5:7; Rev. 5). All Jewish men were required to celebrate Passover in Jerusalem, bringing their families from all over the Roman Empire.

Pentecost—the first day of the Festival of Weeks, this was the fiftieth day (Pentecost) after the Feast of Passover; it was also called "the day of firstfruits" (Num. 28:26), in which people brought a thank offering of new grain to the Lord, the firstfruits of their harvest. For this yearly festival people gathered in Jerusalem from all the Jewish communities scattered around the Roman Empire and beyond (see Acts 2:9-11).

Pharisees—one of three main religious sects at the time of Christ and the apostles. The other two groups were the Sadducees and Essenes. Pharisees emphasized precise obedience to scriptural and traditional law. A number of Pharisees were part of the Sanhedrin, the Jewish ruling council.

Pilate—Roman governor of Judea to whom the Jews brought Jesus for sentencing.

priests—see **Levites**.

proconsul—governor of a Roman province.

prophet—someone who speaks God's message (see Deut. 18:17-19); generally a person who preached God's Word and (in some cases) foretold the future as revealed by the Lord.

repent—to turn back to God out of sorrow for sin.

righteous—considered right with God. As God's people, we are called to be righteous and are credited with Christ's righteousness: we are made right with God through Jesus' death and given the ability to live in right relationships with others through the power of the Holy Spirit (Rom. 3:21-26).

Righteous One—another name for Jesus Christ.

Sabbath—the seventh day of the week (Saturday), set aside as a day of rest and restoration according to the law of Moses.

Sadducees—one of three main religious sects in Jesus' day. They recognized only the five books of Moses as the law of God and did not believe in spirits, angels, resurrection, or life after death. See also **Pharisees**.

Sanhedrin—the ruling council of the Jews, made up of seventy-one officials including Pharisees, Sadducees, leading elders, legal experts, and priests.

Satan—this name means "accuser" (see Zech. 3:1) and refers to the fallen angel who tempted humanity to sin and wants to destroy God's kingdom.

Scriptures—the Jewish Scriptures, which today make up the Old Testament part of the Bible. As a whole, these Scriptures are sometimes called "the Law and the Prophets" in the New Testament (Matt. 22:40; Rom. 3:21), and they consist of the Law (*Torah*, Pentateuch, first five books [of Moses]: Genesis, Exodus, Leviticus, Numbers, Deuteronomy) and books known as "the Prophets" (Joshua through Kings; Isaiah through Malachi) as well as "the Writings" (remaining books of history, poetry, songs, and wisdom literature).

sin—disobedience to God; refers to breaking God's law (1 John 3:4).

Spirit (Holy Spirit)—see **Holy Spirit**.

synagogue—a place where local Jews gathered for religious instruction, worship, and prayer. A synagogue could be organized if a Jewish community had a minimum of ten men.

temple—the religious center of Judaism in the Old Testament and in Jesus' day. Located in Jerusalem, it was the place of worship and sacrifice, the site of major Jewish festivals, and the gathering place of religious thinkers, teachers, and leaders.

How to Use This Study

This Bible study aims to help people engage in lively discussion and learning without having studied the text before doing each lesson together.

Map, Glossary

Near the front of this booklet are maps and a glossary that can be useful for locating places and the meanings of terms mentioned in the book of Acts. Use the map on pages 4-5 to trace the earliest missionary journeys!

Questions for Discussion

The main questions for discussion are numbered and are in bold print. Along with these questions you'll find points "to think about as you discuss" to help spark ideas for responding to each main question. In addition, you'll often see questions that help to connect the story to everyday life under the subheading "What does this mean to me?"

Please do not feel you have to answer every question in the lesson material. Our goal is to help make Bible study a creative, flexible, exploratory exercise in which you engage with your group and grow to know God and each other better.

Follow-up Ideas

At the end of each lesson are Explore! ideas that you might like to use for follow-up. These include activities that can help you learn more about items of interest related to the lesson and apply your learning to everyday life. There are also music and video suggestions.

Break Away (at-home readings)

After the study material for each lesson you'll find readings for use at home. Take a break with God and do some thinking about the lesson material and how the Lord can use it to shape your life. If you like, clip these pages out and set them in places around your home or at work where they can remind you to spend time with God. You might also like to memorize some of the Scriptures used in these pieces.

An Invitation and Prayer of Commitment

If you're searching for a relationship with God, or studying with a friend who is searching, see An Invitation (to believe and commit to God) and a Prayer of Commitment provided at the back of this booklet. These can be helpful in talking one-to-one with God or with someone who is ready to make a faith commitment to God.

Leader's Notes

At the Faith Alive website page featuring this Bible study—see www.FaithAliveResources.org, search for "Acts: Church on the Edge," and click on the link to "Leader's Notes"—you'll find tips for leading this small group study.

We wish you God's blessing as you participate in Bible study together. Have fun as you learn and grow closer to God and one another!

Introduction

The book of Acts picks up where the story of Jesus and his followers leaves off in Matthew, Mark, Luke, and John. As the narrative continues, we discover what happens

- as Jesus goes to the Father (John 16:7; Luke 24:51; Acts 1:9-11),
- as the Holy Spirit comes to Jesus' followers (Acts 1:8; 2:1-41),
- and as the church forms and spreads.

Acts presents the new community of the church in its finest hour—facing struggles and often under attack, but unstoppable with the incredible power and living presence of the Holy Spirit.

The book of Acts was written by Luke, a Greek physician (see Col. 4:14), around A.D. 60-62. Acts is a sequel to Luke's first book, the gospel of Luke, one of the gospel ("good news") accounts that give us the story of Jesus' life and mission. (Note the opening lines in both Luke and Acts, referring to a "Theophilus"; Acts 1:1-3 summarizes what is written in the earlier book;

early Christian writers from the first and second centuries are unanimous in saying Luke is the writer of Luke and Acts.)

We aren't told how Luke became a believer in Jesus, but we do know that he traveled with Paul on some of his missionary journeys. Paul mentions Luke in some of his letters to churches that they planted (Col. 4:14; 2 Tim. 4:11; Philemon 24), and in the second part of Acts, the writer sometimes uses "we" and "us," describing events from his own perspective, showing that he was with Paul during those episodes (see Acts 16:10-17; 20:5-21:19; 27:1-28:16).

In this study we will gain a glimpse into the events and personalities that make up the history of the early church, especially as the Spirit of God works through believers in Christ to bring the good news of God's love and salvation "to the ends of the earth" (Acts 1:8; see John 3:16).

Before you begin . . .

Think of something in your lifetime that began very small but then grew rapidly and took the world by storm (a fad, new technology, political movement, other?). Why did it have such a great influence?

Lesson 1
Anticipation

Acts 1

I picked my young kids up from school one Friday afternoon and told them to pack an overnight bag; we were going on a "surprise ride." At home I heard excitement in their voices as they opened and closed drawers and closet doors to gather their gear.

Back in the car, they were surprisingly quiet, looking for clues as we got onto the freeway and headed north. The anticipation grew as we put miles behind us. Just when they thought they couldn't stand it any longer, they spotted the gigantic sign of a well-known theme park. Shouts of joy and excitement rang out as they realized where we were going. As they recall that day now, the kids laugh about the excitement of the unknown and how much they enjoyed the anticipation that day.

In Acts 1 we find Jesus' followers anticipating the mysterious gift he had promised them. Obediently they suspended "business as usual" and gathered in Jerusalem to wait for this gift, without much of an idea of what it would look like.

~~~~~~~~~~~~~~~~~~~~~~~~~~~~~~~~~~~

Opener (optional)
Share an experience of anticipation that has made an unforgettable impact on your life.

~~~~~~~~~~~~~~~~~~~~~~~~~~~~~~~~~~~

EPISODE 1

Acts 1:1-5
1. What do we learn about Jesus in these opening verses of Acts?
To think about as you discuss . . .
- some of the "convincing proofs" (see Luke 24; John 20-21)
- what it might have been like to be with Jesus at this time
- what Jesus' followers (disciples, apostles) were expecting

See **glossary** for info about **disciples** and **apostles**.

Wouldn't You Be Staring?

In Acts 1:3 the original Greek text for "appeared to them" is *optanomenos autois*, which literally means "being seen by them." Our word *ophthalmologist* ("eye doctor") comes from the same Greek root. Scholars suggest that the use of this word means Jesus was being "eyeballed," "stared at," or "scrutinized" by his followers. If your friend and teacher was crucified and came back to life and now stood before your very eyes, wouldn't you be staring too? The disciples weren't the only ones who stared at Jesus. According to 1 Corinthians 15:6 Jesus appeared to more than 500 eyewitnesses after his resurrection.

2. What did Jesus command the disciples to do, and why?

To think about as you discuss . . .

- the "gift" the Father promised
- baptism with water, baptism with the Holy Spirit (see Matt. 28:19-20; Luke 3:16; 24:46-49)

Acts 1:6-8

3. How does Jesus' view of the kingdom compare to that of the disciples?

To think about as you discuss . . .

- the apostles' hope and expectation (compare with John 6:15; 19:12-15; see also Matt. 20:20-28)
- Jesus' response (see also Mark 1:15; Luke 11:20; 13:18-21; 17:20-21; John 18:36-37)

Baptism

In shipping terms, a ship that is sunk is "baptized," meaning saturated, overcome, filled. How does this image help us when we think about baptism with the Holy Spirit?

In Luke 3:16, John the Baptist says, "I baptize you with water. But one who is more powerful than I will come, the straps of whose sandals I am not worthy to untie. He will baptize you with the Holy Spirit and fire."

When the early Christians spoke of being baptized with the Holy Spirit, they had these things in mind:

- the Holy Spirit gradually changes believers to be like Jesus (2 Cor. 3:18).
- The Holy Spirit fills believers with his presence, giving them power to do God's will, immersing them in the thinking, values, and character of Jesus (Acts 2:4).
- Baptism is also a symbol of being cleansed in Christ (Acts 22:16; 1 Cor. 6:11), and immersion is a symbol of dying and rising with Christ (Rom. 6:3-4).

4. How did Jesus assure the disciples that they would receive the Holy Spirit? How would they be involved?

To think about as you discuss . . .

- the vastness of the mission, and how that might affect the apostles
- what it means to be a witness (see Isa. 43:10-12)

Witness, Martyr?

Our word *witness* comes from an Old English word, *wit*, meaning "knowledge." A witness is someone who can give testimony based on knowledge.

The Greek word that is translated as "witnesses" in Acts 1:8 is *martyres*, from which our word "martyr" comes. **What does this add to our understanding of Jesus' declaration that we will be his witnesses?**

What does this mean to me?

- Where is your Jerusalem, Judea, and Samaria . . . ?

A Handy Outline

The itinerary Jesus establishes becomes the outline for the book of Acts:

- Jerusalem—Acts 1-7
- Judea and Samaria—Acts 8-12
- the ends of the earth—Acts 13-28

Acts 1:9-11

5. Picture and describe what happened next. How do you think this affected the disciples that day? Why was this event important?

To think about as you discuss . . .

- who the "men dressed in white" were (see Matt. 28:1-3; Luke 24:4; John 20:12), how they explained this event, and the promise they mentioned
- why it was good that Jesus went away (see John 16:7-15)

View of the Mount of Olives today as seen from the temple mount in Jerusalem.

What does this mean to me?

- Have you ever found yourself awestruck by a situation or event? What were you feeling? What got you moving again?

- Reflect on some of your favorite promises from God. Describe one and explain how it helps you.

Digging Deeper

The following Scriptures help to explain more about Jesus' ascension:

- Romans 8:31-39
- Ephesians 1:18-23; 2:6; 4:7-16
- Philippians 2:5-11
- Hebrews 1:1-4; 12:2
- Revelation 5

EPISODE 2

Acts 1:12-14

7. What do these verses tell us about Jesus' followers and what they did after Jesus ascended?

To think about as you discuss . . .

- the apostles' activities as they returned to Jerusalem (see also Luke 24:50-53; Acts 1:4)
- age, gender, and other characteristics of the group members
- the fact that some were Jesus' family members (see also Matt. 27:55-61; Mark 3:20-21, 31-35; 6:1-6; Luke 23:49; John 7:1-10)

Apostle Trivia

Not only did several of the apostles have the same first name (Simon, James, Judas—see Luke 6:13-16), but one of them was called "Simon the Zealot."

What was a zealot? In the apostles' day this term referred to someone who had great zeal for the Jewish law and the kingship of God, and who may have belonged to a revolutionary political party that wanted to overthrow the Roman rule in Israel. Though he wouldn't have remained part of that group, Simon the Zealot probably kept his "nickname" to avoid being confused with Simon Peter (see Matt. 4:18; Luke 5:8; John 1:40-42).

Acts 1:15-22

8. What was the apostles' motivation in replacing Judas? What was their main purpose as Jesus' followers?

To think about as you discuss . . .

- Peter's reasoning in verses 17 and 22
- how this connected with Jesus' statement in verse 8

9. What do these verses tell us about Judas?

To think about as you discuss . . .

- how the apostles (as his friends and coworkers) felt about and dealt with Judas's betrayal and death
- other passages about Judas's betrayal and death
  - —Matthew 26:14-16; 27:1-10
  - —Mark 14:10-11, 43-46
  - —Luke 22:1-6, 47-48
  - —John 13:18-30

Acts 1:23-26

10. What was the apostles' solution for replacing Judas?

To think about as you discuss . . .

- casting lots
- qualifications of the replacement (see Acts 1:21-22)

The Death of Judas

In Acts 1:18-19 Luke gives us a gory description of the apostle Judas's death. This account provides some additional details to the description given in Matthew 27:3-10, which explains that the chief priests bought the field on Judas's behalf after Judas, stricken with remorse, returned the "blood money" that they had paid him to betray Jesus (Matt. 27:5-6). Though Matthew doesn't say it, the place where Judas hanged himself and "fell headlong" (Acts 1:18) was apparently the same field bought with the "blood money" and named "Akeldama, that is, Field of Blood" (Acts 1:19; see Matt. 27:8).

See **glossary** for info about **lots (casting lots)**.

More to Think About

- By watching your life, who or what would people say you follow?

Explore!

- Do a character study on some of the "characters" in Acts 1. Go to the library or online and get to know some of the interesting people that spent time with Jesus, such as Peter, John, James, Mary, and the others listed in Acts 1:13-14. Find out what happened to them. What was their part in history? How did they respond to Jesus' commission to go out and be his witnesses? Where did they end up?
- Prepare yourself to be a witness by writing out your personal testimony. Then ask God to open your eyes to opportunities to share it with others.
- On the map on pages 4-5, pencil in lines or circles where Jesus said his disciples would be his witnesses (Acts 1:8). What progression or order do you see in the pattern described by Jesus? What does this show us about the spread of the good news of salvation in Christ?

Break Away (at-home readings)

Take the Best Shortcut

Jesus came to them and said, "All authority in heaven and on earth has been given to me. Therefore go and make disciples of all nations, baptizing them in the name of the Father and of the Son and of the Holy Spirit, and teaching them to obey everything I have commanded you. And surely I am with you always, to the very end of the age."   —Matthew 28:18-20

Before ascending into heaven, Jesus gave instructions to his disciples in three parts. He told them to "go and make disciples . . . baptizing them . . . and teaching them." He was also very clear about what he wanted them to teach: "everything I have commanded you."

Where can we find these teachings today? Well, we can listen to Christian radio, go to a local church, spend time in prayer—these are all helpful in growing spiritually. But reading the Word of God is the best shortcut we can take to get to know Jesus and his teachings. The Scriptures are as relevant in our world today as when Christ walked the earth two thousand years ago.

Do you believe Jesus has "all authority," as he stated in Matthew 28:18? This means he is the ruler of all things in heaven and on earth (Eph. 1:18-23). How can you be more obedient to the ruler of all creation this week?

> Do not merely listen to the word, and so deceive yourselves. Do what it says. . . . Whoever looks intently into the perfect law that gives freedom, and continues in it—not forgetting what they have heard, but doing it—they will be blessed in what they do.
>
> —James 1:22, 25

Is It a Ghost?

He said to them, "Why are you troubled, and why do doubts rise in your minds? Look at my hands and my feet. It is I myself! Touch me and see; a ghost does not have flesh and bones, as you see I have."   —Luke 24:38-39

Acts 1:3 reminds us that after his suffering, Jesus "presented himself" to his disciples "and gave many convincing proofs that he was alive." I hate to admit that I probably wouldn't have been able to believe my eyes if I had seen Christ's body, alive and well, after witnessing his crucifixion. Imagine placing your fingers into the nail-pierced hands of your Savior, to feel the scars left behind, cruel reminders of the agony he endured as he hung on the cross. I want to feel more intensely the awe, the relief, the hope, and the great love the disciples must have felt when they realized Christ had been raised from the dead . . . just as he said he would be. Amazing!

Spend some time today thinking about the pain and suffering Jesus went through as he paid the price for our sin. Thank him for that. But don't stop there. Experience also the joy of knowing that he is alive—and that he promises he will come back again!

Waiting

Wait for the L ORD ; be strong and take heart and wait for the L ORD .

—Psalm 27:14

"The Advocate, the Holy Spirit, whom the Father will send in my name, will teach you all things and will remind you of everything I have said to you."

—John 14:26

Jesus told his disciples to wait for "the gift" the Father had promised (Acts 1:4). They obediently waited, not knowing what this gift would look like. They returned to Jerusalem after Jesus ascended into heaven. While they waited, they prayed and worshiped together. On Pentecost, Jesus' followers were rewarded for waiting when their counselor and comforter, "the Advocate, the Holy Spirit," roared into the room and "what seemed to be tongues of fire . . . came to rest on each of them" (Acts 2:3).

There are times in our lives when we get impatient while waiting for an answer or direction from God. We want to take action and do it our way. This week, let's practice waiting on God.

Worth So Much More

"Are not two sparrows sold for a penny? Yet not one of them will fall to the ground apart from the will of your Father. And even the very hairs of your head are all numbered. So don't be afraid; you are worth more than many sparrows."

—Matthew 10:29-31

Each spring, I welcome the return of many kinds of birds that we feed in our backyard. We put out suet, birdseed, sunflower seeds, and hummingbird feeders. It's such a pleasure to watch the different kinds of birds and to look up unfamiliar breeds in my bird book.

The migration of birds shows that our God is a God of creativity and order. He shaped the ruby-throated hummingbird to weigh less than a coin with wings that beat 60 to 80 times per *second* in normal flight. This tiny bird requires a diet of approximately its weight in nectar or sugar water each day. And yet it migrates back and forth from Canada to Central America, up to 3,200 miles. Experts claim that the ruby-throated hummingbird crosses the Gulf of Mexico, about 525 miles, in an estimated 20 hours of non-stop flight.

When God created "every winged bird according to its kind" (Gen. 1:21), he saw that it was good. Even more, the same creative God who made the hummingbird also designed us human beings and made us in his image. And then, when we fell into sin, God showed that he also had the answer for us to be saved—through Jesus Christ.

What imagination and care there is on display for us in all of life! We truly serve an amazing God.

Strike a Match

If we walk in the light, as he is in the light, we have fellowship with one another, and the blood of Jesus, his Son, purifies us from all sin.

—1 John 1:7

I was touring Mammoth Cave in Kentucky a few years ago with my family. As we entered a chilly underground cavern with a high cathedral ceiling, the guide gathered our group together and turned out the lamp. We were standing in total darkness. My eyes widened but couldn't find any light. We all froze where we stood, afraid to take a step into the darkness. After a few moments, the guide lit a match. I was amazed at how much light one little match had the power to give off. All eyes were drawn to it. I breathed a sigh of relief as I felt the tension in my body release.

God wants to be our light to guide us through life. In Psalm 119:105 God's Word is compared to a lamp that lights our way, illuminating the path we need to follow. If we get ahead of the light, we will stumble and struggle, unable to find the way we need to go.

Do you have big decisions to make? Pray like the disciples did, interact with others, and read God's Word—but also wait on the Lord to show you his will for your life. Do you thirst for the truth of God's Word? Ask God to light your path so that you can find your way in this dark world.

Lesson 2
Power from Heaven

Acts 2:1-41

To start a campfire, it helps to have a fire pit, dry wood, kindling, and—most important—a match! Without that, lighting the fire would be nearly impossible (for most of us). A pile of wood cannot, on its own, produce enough heat to provide warmth, cook a hot dog, or even roast a marshmallow. By simply adding a little flame to dry kindling and wood, we can start a fire that gives heat and light for cooking and for the enjoyment of all who gather around it.

In our study of Acts 2 we will see how the Holy Spirit, the marvelous gift God gave to the church, started a fire that quickly spread and burns ever more powerfully today.

Opener (optional)
Describe an experience you (or someone you know) have had with the power of fire.

Acts 2:1-4

1. Imagine yourself in the surroundings described in these verses. What would you be experiencing (sights, sounds, smells . . . other sensations)?

To think about as you discuss . . .
- where the disciples were, who was present (see Acts 1:13-14), what they were doing, and why (see 1:4)
- what day it was (see Lev. 23:4-16; Num. 28:16-31; "Pentecost" was the fiftieth day after the Passover feast)

A Great Feast, a New Beginning

Jesus promised his disciples that after he went to the Father, his Spirit would come to be with all who believe (John 14:16-17, 26; 16:7-15). This promise was fulfilled on the first day of the Festival of Weeks; that day was the fiftieth day (Pentecost) after the Feast of Passover, and it was also called "the day of firstfruits" (Num. 28:26), in which people brought a thank offering of new grain to the Lord, the firstfruits of their harvest. For this yearly festival people would gather in Jerusalem from all the Jewish communities scattered around the Roman Empire and beyond (see Acts 2:9-11).

Into this festive gathering in Jerusalem the Spirit came, not quietly or calmly but with gusto, with the sound of a violent wind from heaven and "what seemed to be tongues of fire" that lighted on each of the believers (2:3), probably in the same house where they "joined together constantly in prayer" (1:14).

The Holy Spirit empowered Jesus' followers to begin their witness immediately, as they "began to speak in other tongues" so that each visitor to Jerusalem "heard their own language being spoken" (2:6). In this way, everyone could hear the good news of God's salvation through Jesus Christ.

The outpouring of the Holy Spirit on Pentecost marked the beginning of the church as all who believed this good news repented, were baptized, and received the gift of the Holy Spirit (2:38). The presence of the Spirit within a person makes that person a Christian.

2. The Holy Spirit is associated with two symbols in verses 2-3. What are they, and why would these be effective?

To think about as you discuss . . .

- the effects of wind, though it can't be seen, and how it can be helpful, harmful, otherwise (see also John 3:8)
  —other words that describe the attributes of wind
- the effects of fire, and how it can be helpful, harmful, otherwise
  —other words that describe the attributes of fire

Acts 2:5-13

3. Besides the wind and fire, what other phenomenon occurred?

To think about as you discuss . . .

- how this affirmed people of other languages
- how this signaled a reversal of Babel (see Gen. 11:1-9) and that all peoples can be one in Christ

4. What were the reactions of those who heard "the wonders of God" proclaimed in this way?

Of Wind and Fire in the Old Testament

Ezekiel 37:1-14 reveals a vision in which the prophet Ezekiel sees a valley full of dry bones. Then the life-giving breath of God comes as a wind and makes all of the dead bodies alive again.

Exodus 3:2-6 reveals God appearing to Moses on Mount Horeb in the form of "fire from within a bush"—and the fire did not burn up the bush. On that day God called Moses to lead Israel out of slavery in Egypt. After the exodus, the Lord led the Israelites through the desert by way of a pillar of fire at night and a pillar of cloud by day (Ex. 13:21; 40:36-38). At Sinai (Horeb) the Lord came again, descending on the mountain with fire and covering it with a thick cloud of smoke, to give Moses the law for the people (Ex. 19:16-20:21).

See also 1 Kings 18:38-39; 19:11-18.

Countries and Languages Reflected in Acts 2:9-11

Country	Languages and Dialects
Parthia, Media, Elam, Mesopotamia	Aramaic
Judea	Aramaic, Hebrew
Cappadocia, Pontus, Asia, Phrygia, Pamphylia	Local dialects include Phrygian, Pisidian, Lydian, Carian, Lycian, Celtic, Lycaonian, others
Egypt	Coptic
Libya (Cyrene)	Latin (Numidian)
Rome	Latin
Crete	Greek
Arabia	Nabatean (a branch of Aramaic)

Acts 2:14-21

5. How does Peter respond to the people's reactions? What does he explain in these verses?

To think about as you discuss . . .

- Peter's demeanor as he begins speaking to the crowd
- By quoting the prophet Joel (see Joel 2:28-32), Peter was announcing the beginning of the last days. Think about how Peter would have known this prophecy was being fulfilled.

What does this mean to me?

- Reflect on Acts 2:21: "Everyone who calls on the name of the Lord will be saved." How does this motivate you in your personal walk with Jesus? What about your feelings toward unbelievers?

Acts 2:22-36

6. Peter's message to the crowd is centered totally on God's work through Jesus Christ. What can we learn about Jesus from Peter's remarks?

To think about as you discuss . . .
Jesus' ministry (2:22)

- things that happened throughout Jesus' time on earth
- the purpose and focus of Jesus' ministry

The south steps of the temple in Jerusalem, probably the location where Peter preached at Pentecost (Mount of Olives in background).

To think about as you discuss . . .

Jesus' death (2:23)

- who put Jesus to death
- how it affects you to know this was part of God's plan

Jesus' arrest, trial, crucifixion, and resurrection are recorded in all four gospel accounts. See

- Matthew 26:47-28:20
- Mark 14:43-16:8
- Luke 22:47-24:53
- John 18:1-21:25

Jesus' resurrection (2:24-32)

- that death could not keep its hold on him
- that Jesus' death and resurrection were prophesied long before
- that Peter and many others were witnesses of these facts (see 1 Cor. 15:3-8)

Jesus' ascension and exaltation (2:33-36)

- how Peter understood that Jesus was now ruling at the right hand of the Father and that he poured out the Holy Spirit (see John 14:16-17, 26; 16:7-15)
- what it means that Jesus is "both Lord and Messiah" (see Matt. 28:18; Luke 2:11) and why Peter concludes with this statement

Acts 2:37-41

7. How do Peter's listeners react and respond to his message?

- To think about as you discuss . . .
- what it means to be "cut to the heart"
- how a person can receive the gift of the Holy Spirit

See **glossary** for explanations about the terms **Lord**, **Messiah**, **repent**, and **baptism**.

8. Reflect on the promise Peter declares. Whom does it include? Why?

To think about as you discuss . . .

- what this meant for the people who were "cut to the heart," and for their children
- what this means for us and for later generations today

9. Why is it important to continue explaining, warning, and pleading, as Peter did?

To think about as you discuss . . .

- that most people hear the good news many times before they repent and believe and commit their lives to the Lord
- that God calls us many times, not just once, and we sometimes wander and need to be called back
- that continued growth (education, Bible study, worship, fellowship) is needed in our life of faith

What does this mean to me?

- Spend some time reflecting on your response to the Holy Spirit. Have you accepted the Lord's presence in your life?

Explore!

- For some inspirational music that focuses on the Holy Spirit, search for "Holy Spirit songs" at www.YouTube.com.
- Look up names of the Holy Spirit in reference works or on the Internet and reflect on the meanings of these and how they describe the person and work of the Spirit. Some key search terms: Holy Spirit, Counselor, Comforter, Advocate, Spirit of Truth.
- Consider doing a study of the Holy Spirit as a follow-up to this study of Acts. Although this book of the Bible is traditionally known as the Acts of the Apostles, it may be more appropriately named the Acts of the Holy Spirit, as suggested by commentator F. F. Bruce. For small groups that enjoy a discovery (inductive) study method, we recommend *The Holy Spirit: Under the Influence* in the Discover Life series by Faith Alive. Call 1-800-333-8300 or visit www.FaithAliveResources.org for more information.

Break Away (at-home readings)

Joined and Held Together

Speaking the truth in love, we will grow to become in every respect the mature body of him who is the head, that is, Christ. From him the whole body, joined and held together by every supporting ligament, grows and builds itself up in love, as each part does its work.   —Ephesians 4:15-16

California's giant redwood trees grow naturally only in groves on the west coast of the United States. Some of these trees are more than 2,000 years old, and the tallest are more than 370 feet (113 m) high. When you look up into the canopy that filters the sunshine, you can't help staring in awe, but perhaps even more remarkable is the root system hidden under your feet. Redwoods have shallow roots that can spread out to a span of 250 feet. In a grove the tree roots are all intertwined. So each tree is supported by all the others in the grove, making it nearly impossible for them to fall over.

Isn't that something like our new spiritual life in Christ? As we grow, we become more rooted in the truth of Christ, and at the same time we become connected with fellow believers. Together we make up the worldwide body of Christ, the church, with him as our head. And "if God is for us, who can be against us?" Nothing "will able to separate us from the love of God that is in Christ Jesus our Lord" (Rom. 8:31, 39).

Filled, Marked, Guaranteed

When you believed, you were marked in him with a seal, the promised Holy Spirit, who is a deposit guaranteeing our inheritance until the redemption of those who are God's possession—to the praise of his glory.   —Ephesians 1:13-14

My five-year-old granddaughter was helping me make apple pies one autumn day. We peeled the apples, cutting away bad spots and cores, sliced them, and added sugar and spices. As we rolled out the dough, she chatted away about kindergarten and her friends. Our hands got sticky as we filled the pie dishes with apples and covered them with a layer of flattened dough. As we began to seal the edges, I showed her how to put her little finger on the inside rim and pinch the pie dough around it. Her skill improved dramatically as she worked her way around the edge of the dish.

As a final touch, I showed Mia how to cut a design in the top of the pie to release steam as it baked. Then I handed her the knife, and she marked her own pattern in the top of the pie she would take home with her. She looked, with obvious joy, at the finished product. We put the pies into the oven and waited impatiently for them to bake and cool. She was so excited to take her pie home and share it with her family.

I explained to Mia that in some ways pie making is like our relationship with God. God chooses to make us, and he makes us useful for his work by peeling the junk out of our lives. The Spirit fills us, making us fruitful and pleasing to God, and we are marked and sealed with the Spirit as a promise that we can look forward to living forever with God, who loves us.

Have you asked the Creator to fill and seal you with his Spirit? Pray where you are, and he will hear your request. Praise God for his promises and love and the great gift of his Spirit!

A Purpose for Each of Us

The one who has fashioned us for this very purpose is God, who has given us the Spirit as a deposit, guaranteeing what is to come.

—2 Corinthians 5:5

As I enjoyed a cup of coffee outside, I wondered, in a kind of prayer, "God, am I fulfilling the plan you have for me?" The cool fall morning was quiet as I watched leaves drift to the ground all around me. I began to see the leaves individually as they completed their cycle of life, making their way toward eventual decomposition into the ground. Together, the leaves had provided beauty and nourishment for the tree, shaded our backyard from the heat of the sun, and supplied a home and protection for birds, squirrels, and insects. The leaves had fulfilled their purpose, and now, at the end of their season, they were falling to the earth to become compost, providing further nourishment.

God had lovingly provided an example of his great plan by bringing the leaf to my attention. I can glorify God in my everyday life. I can reflect God's love to the people I come into contact with. Together with other Christians, I can be his hands and feet, reaching out to people in need and sharing the truth of God's love and salvation. God created me for a purpose, knows me, and loves me—even though I have been and still am a sinner. At that moment, I felt as if I had been hugged by my creator.

God has a purpose for each of us, in some ways like a *not-so-insignificant* leaf. We may be called to teach, preach, work on the mission field, raise children, or work to the glory of God in some other way (1 Cor. 10:31; Col. 3:23). How can we have assurance that we are fulfilling our purpose? Today, look for evidence that God is pleased with you, and aim to work for the Lord in all you do. Look for ways to find joy in the routine activities of your life, and give praise to God for all good things.

When It's Hard to Love

God demonstrates his own love for us in this: While we were still sinners, Christ died for us.

—Romans 5:8

Teaching an aerobics class several years ago, I had one participant who was exceptionally rude. She interrupted the class continually with her negative comments. It upset me, and I didn't know how to handle the situation. Ignoring her didn't help. Responding to her in a negative way just seemed to encourage her. Several classes later, with her cutting remarks continuing, I decided to pay attention to her, really pay attention. I made a point of greeting her by name and holding a short conversation with her before class. I laughed when she made silly comments. I asked her opinion on the music I was using. I began to see a change in her attitude. By the end of the eight-week session, she had become my most dedicated supporter.

Is there a difficult person in your life? Their behavior may be covering a wounded soul that needs kindness and friendship. Ask God for wisdom in dealing with a difficult person and then deliberately show God's love in words and actions. That's what the Lord did for each one of us—while we were his enemies (Rom. 5:10). What an honor that we can be Christ's hands and feet in a hurting world.

Believing God

"Ask and it will be given to you; seek and you will find; knock and the door will be opened to you. For everyone who asks receives; the one who seeks finds; and to the one who knocks, the door will be opened."
—Luke 11:9-10

I was running late for an appointment. A light on the dashboard came on, saying my gas tank was near empty. *Oh no! I drove yesterday with that light on.* Should I try to make it to my appointment, or should I stop and fill up? Making my decision, I passed by the nearest gas station and continued on. I silently prayed that God would help me in spite of my lack of being prepared. As I pulled into the parking lot, the engine coughed and missed a little. But I successfully parked my car and kept the appointment.

When I returned, a cold drizzle had begun. I prayed again, asking for help despite my own lack of preparation. The engine started up, but as I put the car in reverse, it died. I started it again. While whispering pleas to God, I drove across the busy intersection into another parking lot. Again the engine died. At this point I nearly gave up and walked the quarter mile to the gas station I'd passed earlier, but instead I prayed again.

Against all odds, the engine started up. I put the vehicle in gear and pulled out of the parking lot. I made it all the way to the station and parked near the gas pump, where I actually had to turn the key to shut off the car. *Thank you, God! You are so good to me!*

I know God lovingly provided for me that day. He is intricately involved in our daily lives. Just as parents want to give good gifts to their children, so does God— even despite our foolishness sometimes! That's because he loves us. In my case, God may have been protecting me from some danger I was unaware of. Who knows but the Lord? And I'm thankful. God enjoys our gratitude, praise, and thanksgiving. (This is not to say we should put ourselves in danger to test God, but I did learn in an unforgettable way that the Lord watches over me. See Deut. 6:16; Ps. 121; Matt. 4:7.)

Are you taking your needs to God, no matter how trivial or foolish they may seem? He knows what's in our hearts before we ask. And he loves us and cares for us. Believe that God can display his infinite power in your life.

Lesson 3
The Gift of Boldness

Acts 2:42-4:31

In lesson 2 we learned that about three thousand Jews were baptized and received the gift of the Holy Spirit (Acts 2:41). The early church was beginning to grow in their newfound faith in Christ as well as in numbers. As the new body of believers began their life together in Christ, united by the work of the Holy Spirit in them, wonderful things began to happen.

But, as Jesus had predicted, trouble was not far off (Luke 21:12-19; John 15:18-27). The first followers found themselves in a position that would test their beliefs and force them to stand up boldly for their Savior.

Opener (optional)

Describe a time when you or someone you know stepped up boldly to do what was right.

EPISODE 1

Acts 2:42-47

1. What comes to mind when you think of a community like this one?

To think about as you discuss . . .
- how the believers expressed their oneness and love
- what they felt was important
- their attitude toward sharing
- that they were able to build community even though many of them were not from Jerusalem (see 2:41, 47; 4:4)

"The Lord added to their number . . ." (Acts 2:47). Luke mentions several times that the number of new believers increased—steadily and sometimes dramatically (see 2:41; 2:47; 4:4; 5:14). F. F. Bruce comments, "It is the Lord whose prerogative it is to add new members to his own community; it is the joyful duty of the community to welcome . . . those whom Christ has accepted (cf. Rom. 15:7)." For additional summary statements throughout the book, see Acts 6:7; 9:31; 12:24; 16:5; 19:20; 28:31.

2. Reflect on the four main activities that shaped this community (see Acts 2:42). Why were these significant, and how do we (should we) practice them today?

a. _____.

What did this look like back then?
What would this look like today?

b. _____.

What did this look like back then?
What would this look like today?

c. _____.

What did this look like back then?
What would this look like today?

d. _____.

What did this look like back then?
What would this look like today?

What does this mean to me?

• How do these practices intersect with my life today?

Focus Points of Christian Community

Apostles' teaching—In Matthew 28:19-20 Jesus told his apostles, "Go and make disciples of all nations, baptizing them . . . and teaching them . . ."

Fellowship—The Greek word for "fellowship" is *koinonia* – meaning communion by participation. This involves mutual partnership, interaction, helping one another, sharing, sympathy, communication, caring, welcoming, responsibility, and so on.

Breaking of bread—In most cultures still today there's something about eating together that draws people closer and expresses a desire for unity and goodwill among all who participate. Eating together provides a setting for hospitality, sharing, and caring that strengthen a sense of working together, serving one another, open communication, trust, and peace.

Prayer—Prayer can be defined as communication with God by which we honor him as Lord of our life. In prayer we bring to God all our joys and concerns, showing that we trust him and depend on him for our needs, for direction, and for a growing relationship by which we walk with the Spirit to become more and more like Jesus Christ, our Savior (see 2 Cor. 3:18; Gal. 5:25).

EPISODE 2

Acts 3:1-10

3. Why were Peter and John at the temple, and whom did they see there? Describe what happened.

To think about as you discuss . . .

- why the custom of prayer remained important for the new believers, and what it showed to fellow Jews
- why the lame man was brought to the temple gate each day
- how you would describe this man (see Acts 4:22 for his age)
- what Peter and John could have done instead of stopping
- what the man expected, and what he received
- how Peter acted, on whose authority, and why

4. How did the man react to the miracle? How did the people react?

To think about as you discuss . . .

- how this event provided an opportunity to witness for Christ

What does this mean to me?

- Think of a time when you did not get what you wanted but received what you needed. How did God help you in that situation?

Prayer at the Temple

In those times the Jews customarily went to (or knelt in the direction of) the temple three times for prayer each day (see Dan. 6:10)—the third hour (about 9 a.m.), the ninth hour (about 3 p.m.), and sunset. The temple was the central place of Jewish worship and sacrifice, located in Jerusalem. See **temple** in glossary.

Begging at the Temple

The *NIV Life Application Study Bible* refers to begging at the temple as follows: "Giving money to beggars was considered praiseworthy in the Jewish religion. So the beggar wisely placed himself where pious people might see him on their way to worship at the temple."

See also John 5:1-9, noting Jesus' question and how the man there responded.

Acts 3:11–4:4

5. What does Peter explain in verses 11-26? How is this similar to his speech in Acts 2, and how is it different?

To think about as you discuss . . .

- how Peter tailored the message to connect with this miracle
- what Peter says about his listeners and about God
- Peter's boldness in telling this message

Solomon's Colonnade—The outer courts of the temple in Jerusalem were enclosed by a magnificent series of pillars. The front (east) side of the outer courts became known as Solomon's Colonnade (or Solomon's Porch; see map: Jerusalem in Jesus and the Apostles' Day). Before long, this area became a common meeting place for the early church (see Acts 3:11; 5:12).

What does this mean to me?

- In what ways might God be calling you to stand up and be more bold in your community?

6. Why were Peter and John arrested? Did this cause people to reject their message? Explain.

To think about as you discuss . . .

- legal instructions that the leaders might have tried to use to their advantage (see Deut. 13:1-4), and why that really wouldn't work
- the number of people who joined with the believers

EPISODE 3

Acts 4:5-22

7. What gave Peter the boldness to speak out to the religious leaders? How did the leaders respond? Why?

To think about as you discuss . . .

- the trial and death of Jesus about two months earlier (see Matt. 26:57-27:50; John 18:12-19:30), and how Peter and John may have felt as they remembered those events
- how differently the rulers and elders acted in this trial

8. How did Peter describe Jesus here?

To think about as you discuss . . .

- what Peter said about the religious leaders
- what Peter said about salvation

9. What did the Jewish leaders think of Peter and John? What did they tell Peter and John to do? Why?

To think about as you discuss . . .

- Peter and John's response to the leaders' command
- when it is acceptable to disobey authority

What does this mean to me?

- Share a time when you were so excited about something that you couldn't keep quiet. What if you were ordered not to say anything about it? Could you have done that?

Acts 4:23-31

10. **Reflect on the prayer the believers raised together after Peter and John's release. What can we learn here about the believers and about prayer? Did they receive what they asked for? Explain. (See also Luke 11:9-13; 1 John 5:14-15.)**

To think about as you discuss . . .

- how the believers addressed God at the beginning of their prayer
- the ways they praised God in this prayer
- what they asked for, and did not ask for
- what happened after their prayer

What does this mean to me?

- Are you bold enough to pray that despite a situation of suffering or persecution, the Lord will empower you to be a light for the glory of his name? What does it take for any of us to have such boldness?

Explore!

- Do some research on prayer practices among Christians. On the Internet, for example, you could search with keywords like Christian prayer, Lord's Prayer, ACTS, prayers of the saints, prayer disciplines, and much more. For a six-session Bible-based study for small groups, consider *Discover Prayer* in the Discover Your Bible series by Faith Alive. Call 1-800-333-8300 or visit www.FaithAliveResources.org for more information.
- For a creative prayer activity, write out your own prayer in the pattern found in Acts 4:24-30:
  - Begin with an address like "Dear Lord who rules over all things . . ."
  - Offer praise to God for being the creator, revealer, and decision maker in your life . . .

- Ask God for boldness to speak the truth in love and to stand up for others . . .
- Ask him to reveal his power so that people may believe and come to new life in Christ . . .
- Close with a phrase like ". . . and may your will be done, in Jesus' name . . ." and believe it boldly!

Break Away (at-home readings)

Walking with God

After he became the father of Methuselah, Enoch walked faithfully with God 300 years and had other sons and daughters. Altogether, Enoch lived a total of 365 years. Enoch walked faithfully with God; then he was no more, because God took him away.

—Genesis 5:22-24

Since we live by the Spirit, let us keep in step with the Spirit.

—Galatians 5:25

The other day, as I walked my dog Mardy, it struck me how much my relationship with God is similar. Mardy is always excited to walk with me, and I enjoy walking with him. As we start out, he tugs and pulls on the leash. He'd like to get ahead of me, but I remind him with a quick tug that he needs to set his pace to mine. As long as he walks with me, he will be safe from traffic, from larger dogs, and from getting hopelessly lost. Most of the time he obediently and joyfully walks beside me. But sometimes, if a squirrel or bunny darts off to into the woods as we walk by, he forgets he's with me and breaks into a run. When he reaches the end of his leash, he's reminded that I'm still in charge.

Just as I am excited to walk with God, my King, I know he enjoys walking with me (see Deut. 30:9-10; Isa. 62:1-5). Scripture tells us that Enoch, Noah (Gen. 6:9), and many other believers walked with God (see Job 1:1; Heb. 11). By faith they obeyed the Lord. I want to have that kind of relationship with my Lord. I want to walk daily with my God and believe that he knows better than I do where I should go and what I should do. He doesn't keep me on a leash, but—far better!—God gives me his Spirit so I can keep in step. How's it going in your walk with God today?

All-Knowing God

"'Never again will they hunger; never again will they thirst. . . . For the Lamb at the center of the throne will be their shepherd; 'he will lead them to springs of living water.' 'And God will wipe away every tear from their eyes.'" —Revelation 7:16-17

Nothing surprises God. He knows all, and he will accomplish his will in his time. In Acts 4:11, Peter quotes from Psalm 118:22 to tell the religious leaders, "Jesus is 'the stone you builders rejected, which has become the cornerstone.'" Written about a thousand years earlier, that prophecy was fulfilled in the mission of Christ.

When we struggle with the political climate, the economy, war, broken relationships, illness, lack of work, natural disasters, and more, God is still on his throne. In troubled times this brings me great comfort. "I know that my Redeemer lives" (Job 19:25) and will make all things right in the end. "'For I know the plans I have for you,' declares the LORD, 'plans to prosper you and not to harm you, plans to give you hope and a future'" (Jer. 29:11).

You and I can look forward to a time when God will even wipe away our tears. I can only imagine the King of kings and Lord of lords loving me in such a personal way.

Do you worry about your future? Your children's salvation? Earthquake? Storms? War? Find peace and rest in the God of our salvation. In Matthew 11:28 our Savior says, "Come to me, all you who are weary and burdened, and I will give you rest." That's a promise, and God keeps his promises.

Examples of Faith

Command those who are rich in this present world not to be arrogant nor to put their hope in wealth, which is so uncertain, but to put their hope in God, who richly provides us with everything for our enjoyment. —1 Timothy 6:17

In Hebrews 11, the author describes a number of people who lived "by faith." They are impressive examples. Faith is powerful! Great things have been accomplished in God's strength and "by faith," such as passing through the Red Sea on dry land, toppling the walls of Jericho, routing enemies who mocked God and his people, surviving in a den of hungry lions . . . the list goes on and on.

My youth group leaders, Gary and Florence Butler, lived out their faith in front of me. As foster parents, they raised four troubled teenagers. They opened their humble home to give those boys security, purpose, and all the love they would accept. They praised God in all circumstances, knowing that even when the furnace broke down in their old farmhouse, God would provide the funds needed for a replacement. For example, as they gave that burden over to God, I was able to see God answer their prayers in a surprising way. One day an envelope arrived in their mailbox with the exact amount of cash to pay for the expense.

Is there someone in your life that inspires you to be more obedient? Are you living your life as an example of someone who lives by faith?

A Date with God

They sought God eagerly, and he was found by them. So the LORD gave them rest on every side.   —2 Chronicles 15:15

My life had gotten too hectic. My calendar was so full I couldn't pencil in one more thing. I was getting everything done, but I wasn't doing anything to the best of my ability. Even tasks and chores I used to get pleasure from were becoming no more than items to check off my list.

I wasn't the only one affected by this overload. My husband was feeling neglected. My children were feeling that too. Sometimes they would have to wait for me to pick them up from school because I was running late.

My days were filled with activity, but I was feeling empty inside. After a particularly crazy day, I fell into bed in exhaustion, too tired to read my Bible and pray. A stark realization set in. I was spinning my wheels, and I had lost my focus on God and on my family as well.

I knew I had to set aside some time to spend with my heavenly Father. So I wrote it into my schedule, blocking out a few hours in the afternoon for one-on-one time with God. Assured that God would meet me anywhere, anytime, I selected the coffee shop at a nearby bookstore. I brought my notebook and Bible and prepared to concentrate on my relationship with God. I bowed my head to pray while the voices of others hummed around me. As I jotted thoughts and prayers into my notebook, it didn't take long before the hustle and bustle around me receded into the background. I was soon refreshed, finding peace and joy for my weary heart. God communicated his love to me right then and there. I recommitted my life, schedule and all, to the author of life.

As I left the coffee shop, I was eager to schedule another date with God. My priorities had gotten way out of balance. I knew I had to make some tough choices—to begin to say "no" to some activities and "yes" to a steady diet of God and his Word.

God promises that if we seek him, we will find him. Have you set aside time with God this week?

Oldie but Goodie

"My sheep listen to my voice; I know them, and they follow me."
—John 10:27

My bedside alarm clock is old, large, and cumbersome, but it's extremely dependable. One day my fifteen-year-old daughter Emily was laughing at my outdated clock. She was intrigued by the dial that moved the radio-station indicator across the clock face. As she turned the dial, loud static blared from the speaker until she tuned in a talk-radio program. The voice became clear and distinct. She turned toward me with a surprised look on her face, and we had a good laugh together about my "ancient" piece of equipment. This became a teachable moment with my teenager.

I said that, in a way, my radio dial reminded me of how we listen for God's Word. Just because we're not tuned in doesn't mean he's not trying to communicate with us. We only have to adjust our "dial" and listen carefully for a clear channel between us and God. His message is there for us if we take the time and energy to seek it. We talked about how we could tune in to God by reading his Word, spending time in prayer, listening to wholesome music, and going to worship with God's people.

Have you been in tune with God lately? If not, take a moment to confess and intentionally set aside time for him today . . . and tomorrow . . . and the next day. He's waiting for you and will welcome you with open arms.

43

Lesson 4
Challenges Inside and Out

Acts 4:32-5:42

Imagine being part of a church that is growing by leaps and bounds. A church that started with twelve apostles and little more than 100 others added 3,000 on its opening day (Pentecost) and within a short time had thousands more (see Acts 1:15; 2:41, 47; 4:4). Can you visualize being part of a community in which the extraordinary is normal and miracles are a part of everyday living? The early church in Jerusalem was like that. They enjoyed the miraculous display of the presence and power of God day after day. Souls were saved in abundance as they lived by God's love.

But, as we learned in lesson 3, it wasn't all sunshine and roses. The new believers soon found that when you go all out for Jesus, people who prefer doing things their own way aren't going to like it. In today's lesson we discover some challenges the believers faced from both inside and outside their community. Let's see how they reacted to these things.

~~~~~~~~~~~~~~~~~~~~~~~~~~~~~~~~~~~~~

Opener (optional)
Have you ever been blindsided by someone you thought you knew, or by an event you just couldn't see coming? How did it affect your relationship with God?

~~~~~~~~~~~~~~~~~~~~~~~~~~~~~~~~~~~~~

EPISODE 1

Acts 4:32-37
1. Imagine a place where everyone is wholeheartedly in love with the Lord. What would this look like today?

To think about as you discuss . . .
* the believers' motivation, and how they displayed unity
* what the apostles continued to do
* that no one remained needy among them

How good and pleasant it is when God's people live together in unity!

—Psalm 133:1

44

What does this mean to me?

- What can you do to help people in need in your local community (or beyond)?

Encouraging Role Model (Acts 4:36-37) Often when we encounter Barnabas in the New Testament, he is helping, encouraging, uplifting, and claiming the best for people (see also Acts 9:26-27; 11:22-30; 15:36-39).

Acts 5:1-11

2. Consider Ananias and Sapphira's behavior. How did it compare to the new culture of the Christian community? What was their sin?

To think about as you discuss . . .

- why Ananias and Sapphira were punished in this way
- how Peter learned they were lying
- the power that lay behind this couple's sin
- how people might act similarly today

See 2 Corinthians 8-9 for more Scripture related to **New Testament giving.**

3. What does this passage reveal about the connection between truth and unity in the body of Christ?

To think about as you discuss . . .

- the importance of being an authentic Christian

For an Old Testament story about a similar judgment from God, read the story of Achan in Joshua 7. See also Lev. 10:1-2; Num. 16; 2 Sam. 6:6-7.

What does this mean to me?

- Is there any hypocrisy in your life? Consider (examine) the motivations of your heart. Why do you do (or say) the things you do (or say)? (Meditate privately on Psalm 139:23-24.)

Pause for Prayer

You may wish to spend some time as a group, or individually, asking God to uphold truth within your community of believers. Also ask the Spirit to help you speak and act in truth and with Chrislike love in all situations.

EPISODE 2

Acts 5:12-16

4. Reflect on all the extraordinary events described in these verses. How would you sum them up for someone who hasn't heard of them before?

To think about as you discuss . . .

- the fear that people now had about the church, and the seriousness of commitment
- Peter's role among them (see Matt. 16:13-20; John 21:15-19)
- how the Lord tends to work among us today, now that the church has long been established
- that missionaries note similar kinds of events in places where the good news of Jesus has not been introduced before

Acts 5:17-42

5. Why did the religious leaders arrest the apostles?

To think about as you discuss . . .

- how the religious leaders felt and why
- how the apostles escaped prison, and what they did next (vv. 19-21, 25; see also Jesus' words in Luke 22:52-53; John 18:19-21)

An **angel of the Lord** was a special agent from God who brought messages to God's people and sometimes provided them with supernatural help. See also Matt. 1:20; 2:13, 19-20; Luke 1:11-20, 26-37; Acts 12:7-17.

6. How did Peter and the other apostles respond when the leaders accused them? What did the leaders want to do with them?

7. Explain Gamaliel's message and his reasoning. How did his wisdom on the matter show respect for God and eventually bear out the truth of Jesus' message?

To think about as you discuss . . .

- what Gamaliel cautioned the leaders against
- how the leaders responded to his suggestion

Gamaliel was famous in Judaism, recognized as a great teacher in his day (c. A.D. 25-50). Among Christians, he is best known for his statement here in Acts 5 and for his role as a teacher of Saul (Paul—see Acts 22:3).

8. What effects did their conflict with the religious authorities have on the apostles? Why?

To think about as you discuss . . .

- the ways they defied the Sanhedrin's orders, but obeyed God (see Acts 4:18-20; 5:20-21, 28-32)
- how they were treated (see 4:7, 21; 5:18, 27, 33, 40)
- their attitude and state of mind (see 4:12, 23-24; 5:12, 29-32, 41-42)
- where their strength came from (see 4:8, 31; 5:19, 32, 39; see also Luke 21:12-19)

Flogging

The word for "flogged" in Acts 5:40 is *dero*, literally meaning "flay, skin, thrash." The law governing flogging was given in Deuteronomy 25:1-4, imposing a limit of forty lashes. This may not have been as brutal as Jesus' flogging by the Romans, in which a person was beaten with whips that had sharp pieces of metal or bone attached at the ends. But even a flogging with clean whips was terribly painful, leaving deep scars for life.

9. What can we learn from the apostles' example about coping with criticism and unfair treatment because of Christ? What is our reaction to present-day trials and troubles?

What does this mean to me?

- How can we develop a joyful spirit in spite of or in the midst of our circumstances?

Explore!

- For other biblical passages about trials and testing, look up the following. Ask God to point out specific lessons for you as you read.
  - Genesis 22
  - Job 1-2
  - Daniel 3
  - 2 Corinthians 4:7-18; 11:16-12:10
  - Hebrews 10:32-11:40
  - James 1:2-5, 12; 5:10-11
  - 1 Peter 2:20-21; 4:12-19; 5:10-11
- On the Internet, search "martyrs of the Christian faith" for a variety of resources cataloging believers who have faced persecution for their devotion to Christ. Or check out a copy of *Foxe's Book of Martyrs* or *Jesus Freaks: dc Talk and the Voice of the Martyrs* at www.amazon.com or at a library or retail bookstore.
- Personal reflection—Though we know God is in control of the universe, we often forget that he also has plans for each of our lives. Take a few moments and think about God's complete sovereignty *everywhere* . . . including the hallways of your heart.
  - In what ways is this comforting?
  - Does this make you uncomfortable in any way? Explain.
  - Is God calling you to do something about that? If so, what?

Break Away (at-home readings)

Parenting 101

You were taught, with regard to your former way of life, to put off your old self, which is being corrupted by its deceitful desires; to be made new in the attitude of your minds; and to put on the new self, created to be like God in true righteousness and holiness.

—Ephesians 5:22-24

At a family Christmas gathering, my son Luke, who wasn't walking yet, was sitting on the floor playing with his cousins. My sisters and I watched the boys as we chatted at the table. Luke wanted a horse that Adam was playing with, so he crawled over and grabbed it. He put it instantly into his mouth as he plopped down on his behind. I put on my stern face, told him, "No, no," as I took the toy from him and gave it back to my nephew. Luke wasted no time in going after the horse again. I felt frustrated as I took the toy back, again, and gave him a pat on his chubby hand. Now there were two bawling babies, and the situation was escalating.

My wiser sister stepped in with a cookie for both boys. She smiled and spoke tenderly to them as she removed the disputed item. The crying stopped, and they contentedly munched on their snack. As a new mother, I learned a quick lesson that day. I needed to replace the desired item with an acceptable alternative.

In our living for the Lord, we have to replace old habits and passions with good ones. It's not enough to decide to quit doing something that displeases my Savior. I have to fill the gap with something acceptable and pleasing to him. With the Spirit's help, I can "find out what pleases the Lord" and learn to live wisely (Eph. 5:10, 15). Ask God to reveal to you any areas in your life that need to be renewed.

Avoiding Sin

When tempted, no one should say, "God is tempting me." For God . . . does [not] . . . tempt anyone; but each person is tempted when they are dragged away by their own evil desire and enticed.

—James 1:13-14

God is faithful; he will not let you be tempted beyond what you can bear. But when you are tempted, he will also provide a way out so that you can endure it. —1 Corinthians 10:13

I've come to realize that sin is a result of a process. The story of Achan in Joshua 7 gives a clear example. He was not a helpless victim. He made a chain of sinful decisions that led to destruction.

God had clearly warned the Israelites not to take anything when they conquered Jericho. But when Achan saw a beautiful robe and some silver and gold, he coveted them. When did he think he might wear a Babylonian robe? Or even sell one? After coveting the items, he made the decision to steal them. Then, feeling guilty of his sin, he concealed them in his tent. And he was eventually caught. Sadly, the consequences of Achan's sin affected his wife and family as well as the entire nation of Israel.

Sin can gain a hold on our lives if we don't recognize it for what it is. In the beginning, it can be subtle and look attractive, but the penalty for disobedience is costly. With the help of the Holy Spirit, we must be on guard against the evil one by protecting our hearts and minds.

Are you aware of sin in your life? Talk to your loving Father in heaven, say you're sorry, and ask for his strength to overcome it. We can do all things through him who gives us strength (Phil. 4:13).

Jealousy, Envy

A heart at peace gives life to the body, but envy rots the bones. —Proverbs 14:30

Love is patient, love is kind. It does not envy, it does not boast, it is not proud. —1 Corinthians 13:4

In Acts 5:17 we read that "the high priest and all his associates . . . were filled with jealousy." People get jealous when they see someone as a rival and won't tolerate them. Envy enters in when they want the advantage that they see in a rival and, even worse, want to tear that advantage away.

My friend Yvonne is an attractive, vibrant woman who is good at everything she sets her mind to. Her home is clean and orderly, no matter when you stop in to visit. She is a great cook and has a wonderful sense of humor. I would love to be like her in many ways.

Though I enjoyed spending time with her, I wanted many of her qualities, and there were times when I became jealous and maybe even envious. In my mind I didn't measure up to her standards. For years I fought these feelings that caused a wall to grow between us.

I finally realized I was dealing with serious sin. The Holy Spirit opened my eyes and heart to the fact that I wanted my friend's beauty, talents, and abilities instead of simply appreciating them in her. I got on my knees, with tears, and asked my heavenly Father for forgiveness. God has graciously freed me of that sin. I am free to love Yvonne wholeheartedly.

If you are struggling with jealousy or envy, go to the Lord of lords and ask for his forgiveness and healing. Don't put it off. Know the peace that only God can give.

Tough Love

Whatever is true, whatever is noble, whatever is right, whatever is pure, whatever is lovely, whatever is admirable—if anything is excellent or praiseworthy—think about such things. —Philippians 4:8

Mom was always invoking some wise saying to me and my seven brothers and sisters as we were growing up: "Birds of a feather flock together." "Everything in moderation." "Early to bed, early to rise makes a man healthy, wealthy, and wise." Many of these sayings have come to make sense as I've grown older. Sometimes I hear myself saying them!

Mom often used the phrase "Count your blessings" when we grumbled about anything. She tended to be a very positive person, looking on the bright side of nearly any situation.

At a low point early in my marriage, Mom and I were at the coffee shop. I was giving her a list of my grievances, telling her how *my* needs were not being met by my young husband. It's not that he was abusive or hurtful; it's just that he wasn't supplying everything I wanted him to. She let me go on and on, listening patiently to my complaints. When I had finished, she wisely and lovingly put me in my place. She told me I needed to change my focus and look for the good in him.

Well, Mom has been gone now for 22 years, and her example still influences my life today. I'm still married to the same wonderful man, and we will celebrate our 35th wedding anniversary this year!

Take out a pen and paper (literally!) and list your blessings. Thank God for each one. Throughout the day, as they come to mind, thank him again. Remind others to do the same; it can do wonders for their relationships.

Build Someone Up

He died for us so that . . . we may live together with him. Therefore encourage one another and build each other up.
—1Thessalonians 5:10-11

My husband and I, along with a few of our early-bird children, have a tradition of going out for breakfast on Saturday mornings at a local restaurant. It's a great time for us to reconnect. Most of the customers know each other, and the waitress greets us with a cup of coffee and knows our usual order. It makes us feel welcome and comfortable.

One Saturday we noticed an unfamiliar couple sitting at a table by the window. Later we also noticed they weren't talking but were intently texting on their cell phones. We joked that maybe they were chatting (or even arguing) with each other by text message. But then my heart became heavy. There was no real communication going on. No eye contact, expressionless faces turned to their electronic devices. They eventually put their phones down to eat their breakfast. I was sad about their missed opportunity to relate to one another, right there, within arm's reach.

According to some studies, loneliness is on the rise in our culture. But in the new community of Christ, with God's grace and power at work (Acts 4:33), there is a place for everyone. In the strength of Christ, our head, "the whole body, joined and held together by every supporting ligament, grows and builds itself up in love, as each part does its work" (Eph. 4:15-16).

Is there someone you can reach out to with Christ's love today?

Lesson 5
Growing Pains

Acts 6:1-8:1a

Have you heard the story about a hound sitting by the entrance to a small country store? Hour after hour, the dog lay on the dusty old porch. The only thing it managed to do was howl, moan, and groan. A visitor came in and asked the storekeeper, "What's the matter with the dog?"

"He's got a burr stuck on his hind leg," replied the clerk.

"Why doesn't he get it off?" the man asked.

"He'd rather sit and holler," came the response.

Do you have a "burr" bothering you? If so, would you rather have the discomfort of a problem or try to solve it? In this lesson we find that although the early church has been growing in amazing ways, it is also facing difficulties. Next the believers encounter a problem in which they have two choices: do nothing . . . or begin to work things out.

Opener (optional)
How do you usually deal with a problem? (Try to solve it yourself? Seek others' help? Ask God for wisdom? Ignore it and hope it will go away? Some other option?) Why?

Acts 6:1-7
1. Here we read of a problem that threatens to undo the unity of the church in a time of great growth. How is the problem solved?

To think about as you discuss . . .
- the needs that had to be addressed
- the response and the solution offered by the apostles
- how the group responded to the idea

Widows of Hellenistic Jews? Hebraic Jews?

In those days a woman whose husband died was often left destitute, because women were generally not allowed to own property and became dependent on their nearest male relative. Caring for widows (and orphans) was always a special concern of the Lord in the history of God's people (see Deut. 10:17-18; 24:17-22; 27:19; Isa. 1:17, 23-25; Jer. 7:3-7; 22:3). The *NIV Study Bible* describes "Hellenistic Jews" as "those born in lands other than the Holy Land and who spoke the Greek language and were more Grecian than Hebraic in their attitudes and outlook," and it describes "Hebraic Jews" as "those who spoke Palestinian Aramaic and /or Hebrew and preserved Jewish culture and customs." Many Jewish widows who had no other support came from various lands to Jerusalem (see Acts 2:9-11) to live out their final years near the temple. The church included them in its distribution of food to the poor.

2. The seven who were chosen to lead in caring for needy members were selected deliberately and commissioned with this responsibility. What do these verses tell us about them?

To think about as you discuss . . .

- why the apostles didn't volunteer to be the solution
- the importance of the "ministry of the word" and the importance of "service ministry"
- the gifts and talents of the seven who were chosen
- the results for the whole church

The seven "service leaders" are highly commended as being "full of the Spirit and wisdom" (Acts 6:3), but additional details on them are minimal. Nicolas was a Gentile convert to Judaism (6:5). Stephen was "full of God's grace and power" and "performed great wonders and signs" (6:8; see also 6:5). Philip (not the apostle) became an evangelist (one who spread the good news of Jesus) and also did miraculous signs (8:5-7); he also had four daughters who prophesied (21:8-9). We find no further details about Procorus, Nicanor, Timon, and Parmenas. Scholars note, however, that all of the seven had Greek names. The *NIV Study Bible* explains, "The murmuring had come from the Greek-speaking segment of the church; those elected to care for the work came from their number so as to represent their interests fairly."

What does this mean to me?

- What abilities do you have that can be used in service to others? What do you enjoy doing that might help the church and your community?

The Greek word for "wait on" in Acts 6:2 is *diakonein* (literally, "to serve"), from which our word *deacon* comes. The noun form of this word can also be translated as "minister" or "servant."

3. What can we learn here from the early church leaders about resolving differences and solving problems?

To think about as you discuss . . .

- causes of tension and disagreement in churches today
- what happens when believers criticize and argue with one another
- the character traits believers need to get along with one another
- how best to cultivate these qualities (see 1 Cor. 13; Gal. 5:22-25)

Acts 6:8-15

5. How did Stephen get summoned to appear before the Sanhedrin, the ruling council of the Jews?

To think about as you discuss . . .

- the people who argued with him and couldn't stand up to his wisdom (see box; see also Acts 5:17)
- the use of false witnesses (see also Mark 14:55-65)

Synagogue of the Freedmen

"Freedmen" were people freed from slavery and were usually very poor. A group of them from several Hellenistic (Greek-culture) areas had formed a synagogue (a worshiping community that could be constituted with a minimum of ten Jewish men). Because Stephen distributed food to the poor among Greek-speaking Jews like himself, his work would naturally bring him into contact with the Freedmen synagogue. The men of this synagogue began arguing with Stephen and stirring up trouble against him (Acts 6:9-14).

6. Describe Stephen's character and appearance. What would you think of him? Have you ever met a person like him? Explain.

Acts 7:1-53

If time permits, read the entire speech Stephen made to the Sanhedrin. Or see the summary below . . .

In his speech to the Sanhedrin, Stephen makes important points regarding Moses, the law, and the temple, showing that he has not spoken "blasphemous words against Moses and against God," as the false witnesses have claimed (Acts 6:11). Stephen defends his faith by looking back and explaining God's work among Israel's ancestors. Doing so, he gives his listeners—and us—an insightful synopsis of Israel's history.

Stephen shows that God worked through Abraham, Isaac, Jacob, Joseph, Moses, Joshua, David, and Solomon to fulfill his promises and make a dwelling place for his name among his covenant people, Israel. Stephen also points out that

- the Israelites received God's Word, the law, but refused to truly honor the Lord and obey him (7:39).
- they often went through the motions of worship and followed the rules of the law (legalism) but ignored the heart of the law: to love God above all, and their neighbors as themselves (see Deut. 6:4-7; Mic. 6:1-8; Matt. 22:37-40).
- though God was pleased to have the temple in Jerusalem as his dwelling place, a house made by humans could not contain the Lord of heaven and earth (Acts 7:48; see Matt. 18:20; John 4:21-24; Acts 17:24).
- when God sent his prophets to speak his word to the people, the religious leaders persecuted and killed them—and they did the same to Jesus Christ, the Righteous One (Acts 7:52).
- even the sign of circumcision pointed to a circumcision of the heart, in which God writes his law on people's hearts and minds by the Holy Spirit (Acts 6:51; see Deut. 30:6; Jer. 31:33; Rom. 2:28-29; Heb. 8:10).

Stephen then concludes by saying the Jewish leaders (Sanhedrin) have also "received the law . . . but have not obeyed it" (Acts 7:53).

7. Stephen's words resonate with the truths Jesus taught. In what ways has he clarified Israel's story for you?

Acts 7:54-8:1a

8. Why did Stephen's speech infuriate the religious leaders?

To think about as you discuss . . .

- the history of failure, on the people's part, to honor and obey God
- the tradition of legalism upheld by the leaders, ignoring God's law of love (see Matt. 22:34-23:39)
- the Spirit of truth in Stephen, who was now speaking as a prophet they wanted to kill (see John 16:7-15; Acts 7:51-53)

9. How did Stephen face his impending death? Where did he look? What did he see?

To think about as you discuss . . .

- why Stephen was able to face his death so courageously
- how his example can encourage us
- what Stephen saw and why this is significant

Historians note that **"Into your hands I commit my spirit"** was a bedtime prayer commonly learned by Jewish children (see Ps. 31:5).

10. Look and see how Stephen's last words mirrored the final words of Jesus on the cross.

- In Luke 23:46, Jesus prayed . . .

- In Acts 7:59, Stephen prayed . . .

- In Luke 23:34, Jesus prayed . . .

- In Acts 7:60, Stephen prayed . . .

Bible translators note that some early manuscripts of the book of Luke do not include Jesus' words in Luke 23:34. But the statement there is consistent with Jesus' teachings about love and forgiveness of enemies and persecutors (Matt. 5:43-48).

Scholars also explain that Stephen's prayer in Acts 7:60 contrasts with the dying words of a priest, Zechariah, in a similar situation (see 2 Chron. 24:17-22).

What does this mean to me?

- Think of a situation in which you received God's help during a difficult time. What happened? Where did you look for strength? Yourself? Others? God? Did the event help to shape your faith? Explain.

11. What do we learn about Saul in these verses? (Acts 7:58; 8:1a)

Scholars suggest that Saul, who was from Tarsus in Cilicia (Acts 9:11; 21:39; see 8:9), was likely part of the "opposition [that] arose . . . from . . . the Synagogue of the Freedmen" (6:9), probably as one who connected with others in that synagogue who were from Cilicia. Saul (also called Paul—13:9) was also a member of the legalistic Jewish sect known as the Pharisees (23:6; 26:5), whom Jesus had often criticized for losing sight of the heart of God's law of love (Matt. 22:34-23:39; see also John 11:45-53).

Explore!

- Find another translation of the Bible (one that you typically do not use) and read the book of Acts up to this point. (You might also try *The Message*, a paraphrase in contemporary English.) Try to complete your reading in one sitting. Take a few moments to thank God for the story so far and ask for his continuing blessing and revelation as you go forward.
- On the Internet, search "Faith of the Martyrs" and "The Martyrs – Jesus Freaks" for thought-provoking video and commentary on the challenge of facing persecution for Christ, as experienced by Christians through the centuries and in our world today.
- Look back to the Explore! section of lesson 4 for additional follow-up ideas, in case you didn't have time for those earlier.

Break Away (at-home readings)

What Matters Most

I eagerly expect and hope that I will in no way be ashamed, but will have sufficient courage so that now as always Christ will be exalted in my body, whether by life or by death. For to me, to live is Christ and to die is gain.   —Philippians 1:20-21

Stephen was one of the seven leaders appointed to look after the needy in the early church (Acts 6:1-6). He is described as "a man full of faith and of the Holy Spirit" (6:5). He not only helped to provide for the poor; he also "performed great wonders and miraculous signs among the people" (6:8). We also know he received great wisdom from the Spirit, and that his faithfulness to the Lord resulted in his being the first in the early church to die for Jesus' sake (7:59-60).

Other than these things, though, we know little about Stephen. We don't know what he looked like, where he was from, who his parents were, how he made a living, if he was married, if he had children, and so on.

But we do know what was in Stephen's heart. The Spirit of God began living in him and made him a powerful witness for the truth, the good news of Jesus Christ (see Acts 1:8 again). (The Greek word for "witness," by the way, is *martyra*, from which we also get our word *martyr*.)

How do you usually assess a person? Isn't it odd that we can know lots of details about a person's life and yet not know what, or who, is in their heart? What matters most is what's in the heart—the core of our being. And even though I am someone the Spirit is working on, and people might be able to see some fruit of the Spirit produced in me (John 15:1-17; Gal. 5:22-25), it's not about me—it's about the Spirit of Christ working in me.

Is it your goal in life that when your time on earth is through, you will be remembered for your identity in Christ? Financial gain, possessions, status—all that will be left behind. We must focus on what is eternal, living for the one who gives eternal life.

Who Is Your Role Model?

In everything set . . . an example by doing what is good. In your teaching show integrity, seriousness and soundness of speech . . . .

—Titus 2:7-8

"I want to be like her," I commented as we were leaving a restaurant. My husband and I were dating back then, and I'd noticed a sweet little old woman wearing a classy yet simple winter coat and a striking hat as she waited with her husband to be seated.

I caught her eye, and she broke into an engaging smile. Within a few moments I had assessed this aged yet beautiful woman with a peaceful, sweet demeanor, and knew she had something I wanted. After living a long life, she still had a sparkle in her eye and a posture that conveyed spunk and energy.

In my twenties at the time, I thought life didn't get any better, that it would soon be all downhill from there. But that brief encounter gave me hope for growing older. I didn't realize then that the best was yet to come.

Now that I'm a little older, I am still looking to and admiring people that are a generation or two ahead of me. Today I will attend the funeral of an older woman who has affected my way of thinking in a positive way. I came to know Patsy when she was in her fifties and full of life. Laughter erupted from her easily. She was so generous with her time and talents. Filled with the Holy Spirit, she taught Bible studies and mentored younger women. I went on several mission trips with her. Together we folded clothing at a thrift store in Kentucky, painted walls in a classroom, handed out rice and beans to villagers in Honduras, and taught Bible school to enthusiastic children. Her joy was contagious, and her faith was inspiring. Today we will celebrate her life as well as her going home. Praise God!

Look for examples of the person you want to become. Is there someone that has made a positive impact on your life? Thank God for that person, and consider writing a thank-you note to him or her. Are you, in turn, living a life that others would like to aspire to? Our actions and attitudes are picked up by others, whether good or bad. Let's be deliberate in our attempts to learn from older, wiser folks, and to be an example for others.

Lifting One Another Up

Is anyone among you in trouble? Let them pray. Is anyone happy? Let them sing songs of praise. Is anyone among you sick? Let them call the elders of the church to pray over them and anoint them with oil in the name of the Lord.   —James 5:13-14

A dear friend, Dave, was diagnosed with cancer. His doctors agreed on a plan to remove the tumor as soon as possible and then treat with chemotherapy. Our church family, hearing the startling news, pulled together and supported him and his family emotionally and in prayer. At the next Sunday worship service, Dave was called to the front of the church. We were encouraged to come forward to lay hands on him and offer up prayers for healing. As I stood in the crowded circle, reaching in to touch Dave's shoulder, I was moved by the sincere, caring prayer of the body of believers.

After Stephen and six others were chosen to help people in need, "the apostles . . . prayed and laid their hands on them" (Acts 6:6). This gesture of support and blessing is mentioned often in Scripture. In the Old Testament it often symbolized passing along an inheritance to the next generation. It was also used to bestow the gifts and rights of an office, such as priesthood. In the New Testament Jesus laid his hands on little children and prayed for them (Matt. 19:13). He also healed the sick and raised the dead by laying his hands on people (Luke 4:40; 8:54; 13:13).

The next week, Dave joyfully reported that his doctors had decided to take another ultrasound before surgery and, miraculously, found no trace of a tumor! All glory and praise go to the Lord, who heals our diseases. Our faith was strengthened by the healing that took place in Dave's body.

Are you suffering from pain, illness, grief, or perhaps an addiction? The comfort of prayer support by the body of Christ has been a blessing to countless believers. Even if you're not in good health right now, what stories can you share with others about God's care and times of healing in your life? Do you know someone who could benefit from God's healing mercy? Sometimes God chooses to heal us after we depart this life, but most of the time God chooses to heal us here and now.

Protected from Doing Nothing

"Remain in me, as I also remain in you. No branch can bear fruit by itself; it must remain in the vine. Neither can you bear fruit unless you remain in me. I am the vine; you are the branches. If you remain in me and I in you, you will bear much fruit; apart from me you can do nothing."   —John 15:4-5

It was time for a "spiritual checkup." I had been feeling down in the dumps. My zest for living had faded; my outlook on life was dismal. I found myself getting angry over trivial things. I began spending more and more time on the computer in my office, avoiding my family. Negative thoughts plagued me all day long.

This wasn't the first time I'd experienced these symptoms. Over the years I have come to recognize these warning signs. I knew I needed to go to my Healer for the cure. He is the giver of all good things, and at the moment, I was dwelling on the bad.

I opened the Bible to my favorite praise psalm and read, "Praise the Lord, my soul; all my inmost being, praise his holy name. Praise the Lord, my soul, and forget not all his benefits—who forgives all your sins and heals all your diseases, who redeems your life from the pit and crowns you with love and compassion, who satisfies your desires with good things so that your youth is renewed like the eagle's" (Ps. 103:1-5).

We have a choice, daily, to walk with God or to try doing things our own way. At times I believe my way is better, more attractive, easier. But then I am in danger of doing nothing to serve my Lord. That was the problem the religious leaders had when they persecuted Jesus and his followers. That's why they became furious with Stephen, who pointed out their error, and they stoned him to death (Acts 7:51-8:1a).

I thank the Holy Spirit for continually drawing me back to the Lord and to the truth of his Word. The Spirit, working in our hearts, points us to Jesus daily and gradually transforms us to be like him (2 Cor. 3:18).

Isn't that comforting? Picture yourself being cared for, watched over, and protected by the Lord of heaven and earth each day.

A Time to . . .

There is a time for everything, and a season for every activity under the heavens: a time to be born and a time to die . . . .

—Ecclesiastes 3:1-2

In my high school English class, Mrs. Rynberg gave us an unusual homework assignment. She wanted us to write our own obituary. I could hardly believe it! At 16, the last thing I wanted to think about was the end of my life. It seemed morbid and stupid.

I didn't take the assignment seriously. I wrote about being famous as a sports hero who lived a long and very happy life, leaving all of my possessions to my much-loved cat.

I think I understand now what Mrs. Rynberg was hoping to accomplish by that assignment. I think she wanted us to ponder how the decisions we make in our youth can affect the outcome of our lives, the legacy we will leave when we depart this world. She probably wanted us to set goals and dream about the possibilities of our future.

Mark Twain once said, "Life would be infinitely happier if we could only be born at the age of eighty and gradually approach eighteen." That's an interesting thought. Of course, he was talking about having the wisdom of experience while young, so that we could make better decisions than we tend to make at that age. If that were the case, we'd probably make fewer mistakes, and we might take more risks, love more deeply, and live more joyfully in the moment.

Without the Lord, though, I'm sure we'd mess things up just as badly as we do in life the way it is. I'm thankful we have the Holy Spirit to work on us as we go through this life from youth to old age.

After all, God is the one who "set eternity in the human heart" (Eccles. 3:11), and he "is able to do immeasurably more than all we ask or imagine, according to his power that is at work within us" (Eph. 3:20).

God did that with Stephen and with all the other believers who have followed Jesus. Are you ready for him to work that way in you too?

Lesson 6
Interrupted

Acts 8:1b-9:31

The new believers find themselves mourning deeply as they try to sort out the circumstances surrounding the tragic death of their friend and fellow believer, Stephen. They can see clearly that standing up for Jesus can easily result in some type of persecution . . . even death.

In this lesson we meet up with more people who give their attention to the church of Jesus Christ. And in different ways they are interrupted to move in new directions for Christ, as the Spirit moves (see John 3:8).

Opener (optional)
What kinds of interruptions do you like? Explain.

EPISODE 1

Acts 8:1b-4

1. Describe the situation that followed Stephen's death. How could God use this turn of events to spread his salvation message?

To think about as you discuss . . .
- the buildup of opposition that led to the death of Stephen (Acts 7:54-8:1a; see also 4:1-22; 5:17-42; 6:9-15)
- Jesus' commission to the disciples in Acts 1:8
- the systematic violence used by Saul (see also Matt. 16:18)

What does this mean to me?
- What do believers in Christ face today that could be considered opposition or persecution?

2. **"Those who had been scattered preached the word wherever they went" (v. 4). In other words, people were threatened and becoming refugees because of their faith in Jesus—and yet they kept preaching the message of God's salvation in Christ. What does their example teach us? What motivated them?**

To think about as you discuss . . .
- how opposition can draw attention to a movement
- how faithful believers could use this "bad news," by the power of the Spirit, to spread the good news of Jesus

Out of their comfort zone? What comfort zone?

Some interpreters have said that the persecution and scattering of the believers was God's way of pushing them out of their comfort zone in Jerusalem to fulfill Jesus' command to spread the good news to "Judea and Samaria, and to the ends of the earth" (Acts 1:8). But the Bible doesn't support that assessment. Jerusalem had not been a comfort zone for the believers since Jesus was arrested and crucified. Opposition to the believers had been constant. They huddled together in fear until the Holy Spirit gave them boldness and wisdom to preach the good news in all kinds of languages on Pentecost (Acts 2). Then, even though thousands of Jews joined with the small group of believers, the apostles were arrested and questioned on several occasions. The facts show that opposition kept growing to a point where it exploded and people had to run for their lives.

God did not create this opposition or use it to push faithful believers into terrifying circumstances. The opposition to God's kingdom had been here since the beginning of human sin, and now that God's kingdom was coming in a big way, the opposition was fighting back—ferociously. Jesus had predicted this, and the apostles—who did not flee but remained in Jerusalem—understood (Luke 21:12-19; John 15:18-16:33). In conclusion Jesus had said, "I have told you these things, so that in me you may have peace. In this world you will have trouble. But take heart! I have overcome the world" (John 16:33).

The opposition, as it turned out, was no match for the power of the Holy Spirit. Turning the results of opposition into opportunity, the Spirit *continued* to spread the good news of the kingdom of God. Despite the "bad news" of opposition, the believers, filled with the peace and new life of Christ, shared the good news of Jesus "wherever they went" (Acts 8:4).

Acts 8:5-25

3. Philip was one of the seven leaders who had been chosen to minister to the poor in Jerusalem (see Acts 6:5). Where did he go, and what happened when he got there?

To think about as you discuss . . .

- why Samaria was an unexpected place to spread the good news, considering the stormy history between Jews and Samaritans

Who were the Samaritans?

It's important to know that the Jews and Samaritans had despised one another for hundreds of years (see John 4:9). The problem was rooted in long-standing religious differences. Back in 722 B.C. when the Assyrians captured Samaria, they deported many Israelites and replaced them with people from Assyria and neighboring countries. As a result, the worship of God in the region of Samaria became mixed with the religions of other peoples, at least for a time (see 2 Kings 17). The Samaritans, however, insisted that they were the true worshipers of God and that the Jews were heretics who had rejected the holy place of worship on Mount Gerizim established by their ancestors (see Josh. 8:33; John 4:19-20).

Later, after the people of Judah were exiled to Babylon and were set free to return and rebuild Jerusalem, tensions resurfaced. At first some of the Samaritan leaders offered to help rebuild the temple in Jerusalem, but the Jewish leaders refused. As a result, corrupt leaders in Samaria tried to have the rebuilding stopped (see Ezra 4). All this led to further hostility that continued for hundreds of years and was still festering in Jesus and the apostles' day.

Because of this hostility, most Jews would avoid going through Samaria whenever they traveled. To go to Galilee from Judea, for example, Jews would cross the Jordan River and travel along the east bank, and then cross back when they got near the Sea of Galilee. Now, because of the Holy Spirit, the region of Samaria became a destination, just as it was for Jesus when he went there to bring the good news of the kingdom of God (see John 4:4-42).

—adapted from *Discover John: The Word Became Flesh* by Brent and Diane Averill (Faith Alive, 2005).

4. How did Simon the sorcerer try to gain the power of the Holy Spirit? Why? How did Peter respond?

To think about as you discuss . . .

- the spiritual opposition presented by Simon the sorcerer

The Mystery of Simon Magus

Simon the sorcerer (a magician, or magus) presents a mysterious problem in that he believes "the good news of the kingdom of God" and is baptized (Acts 8:12-13) and yet his "heart is not right before God," as noted by Peter later (8:21). Simon's heart problem shows up when he offers to buy the gift of the Holy Spirit (8:18-19). Peter rebukes him and urges him to repent and pray for forgiveness. Peter can see that Simon is "full of bitterness and captive to sin" (8:23). Simon's difficulty is that he is deeply enslaved to the sinful nature (see John 8:31-36), having dabbled in sorcery and occult practices—forbidden by the Lord because of their powerful danger to people's souls (Lev. 19:31; 20:6, 27; Deut. 18:9-13). For a long time Simon has given his heart to the powers of evil, and he apparently is not willing to put off the sinful nature and turn his heart over completely to God (see Col. 3:5-17; 1 Tim. 3:1-7). Instead, he likes what he sees in the power of God and wants to use it for himself. After Peter rebukes him, Simon asks Peter to pray for him, that he may not perish (see 8:20).

Though we hear no more about Simon the sorcerer or whether he further repented, the warning is clear: the power of God is not for sale. Salvation from sin is free to all who believe in Christ as Lord and Savior, whose shed blood fully paid the price, once for all (Heb. 10:10-14), to set us free from captivity to sin.

Acts 8:26-40

5. How does God interrupt Philip's ministry and spread the good news of Jesus in a different direction? What does this tell us about God's love for all people?

6. How does Philip make himself available to the work of the Spirit and to the person he meets? When does the opportunity to share the good news become clear? What are the results?

To think about as you discuss . . .

- Philip's obedience, though he doesn't know what the Spirit intends
- the opportunity to meet with a Gentile worshiper of God who is on his way home to a distant land south of Jerusalem
- what that means for the spread of the good news

What does this mean to me?

- Are you available to share the good news as the Spirit leads you? Explain.

The Way

In Acts 9:2 we find the first biblical reference to "The Way" as a name for the followers of Jesus, and it occurs several times only in the book of Acts (see 16:17; 18:25-26; 19:9, 23; 22:4; 24:14, 22). The name is not explained, so it was apparently well known to Luke's first readers. It probably came from Jesus' description of himself as "the way and the truth and the life" (John 14:6). (See also 2 Pet. 2:2.)

EPISODE 2

Acts 9:1-19a

7. Our story in Acts picks up again on Saul and his persecution of the church. How does the Lord interrupt Saul in his "mission"?

To think about as you discuss . . .

- the energy and intensity of Saul on his mission against the Way
- how Saul was affected by his encounter with Jesus

8. How does the Lord's work with Saul interrupt Ananias?

To think about as you discuss . . .

- Ananias's character
- his hesitation at first, and his obedience
- the Lord's response and explanation

9. What happens when Ananias trusts the Lord and obeys?

To think about as you discuss . . .

- how Ananias treats Saul
- what happens to Saul and how he responds

Entrance to Straight Street in Damascus, where Ananias met Saul.

10. **God has a way of stretching us—and sometimes even breaking us—to remake us. How was Saul remade? What about Ananias? What about you?**

Acts 9:19b-31

11. **What does Paul do now for Jesus, and how is he treated? How is he protected? How does this help the church?**

To think about as you discuss . . .

- Saul's surprising turnaround and energy to promote Jesus
- the threats on Saul's life, and who helps him
- Barnabas's support (see Acts 4:36)
- Luke's summary in verse 31 (see again Acts 1:8)

Explore!

- Look through the following passages for biblical terms associated with conversion and coming to new life in Christ. Use what you've learned to come up with a definition that makes sense to you. The passages: Jeremiah 31:23-34; John 1:12-13; 3:3-8, 16; Acts 16:13-15; Romans 5:10-11; 10:9-10; 2 Corinthians 5:16-21; Ephesians 2:1-10; 1 Thessalonians 1:9-10; 1 Timothy 3:6; Titus 3:4-8; 1 Peter 2:9-10; 1 John 3:9
- Spend some time reflecting and write your own personal testimony. Describe your life before and after the Spirit of Jesus came into your heart. Then find someone to share it with!
- On www.youtube.com search for drama and music videos about Saul and conversion by searching "Saul of Tarsus," "Amazing Grace," "Lord, I Want to Be a Christian," and similar terms.

Break Away (at-home readings)

Just Say Yes

"Surely God is my salvation; I will trust and not be afraid. . . ." With joy you will draw water from the wells of salvation.　　　　—Isaiah 12:2-3

Philip was one of the appointed leaders we read about in Acts 6. After Stephen was stoned to death, most of the believers scattered throughout Judea and Samaria. Philip preached in Samaria, and "when the crowds heard Philip and saw the signs he performed, they all paid close attention to what he said" (Acts 8:6).

Philip was filled with the Holy Spirit and was walking closely with God. Then one day an angel of the Lord told Philip, "Go south to the road—the desert road—that goes down from Jerusalem to Gaza" (Acts 8:26).

Wow—imagine having an angel of the Lord speak to you! And what follows is just as astounding. The next verse says, "So he started out." Philip obeyed, apparently without any hesitation.

Philip's example encourages me in my journey of faith. Are you ready to trust God and obey his leading? What do you have to lose? What do you have to gain?

Contagious Faith

Many of the Samaritans from that town believed in him because of the woman's testimony.　　　　—John 4:39

Jesus encountered many people during his preaching and teaching ministry. He was able to transform lives in many ways—by a conversation, by his presence, by preaching, through healing. John 4 tells of Jesus meeting a Samaritan woman at a well. Much of the chapter is devoted to this meeting and how it influenced an entire area. Jesus, being the Son of God, knew all about her life. She had had many failed marriages and was currently living with a man who wasn't her husband.

Without accusation or judgment, he offered her a better way. She was curious about the "living water" that Christ could give. Before they parted, she learned that he was the Messiah everyone had been waiting for.

She was so transformed by this brief meeting with Jesus that she couldn't keep it to herself. She must have told nearly everyone she met back in town that day. Many of them wanted to meet him as well.

Scripture doesn't tell us her name. We don't know what happened to her after that life-altering meeting with Christ. But we do hear about the impact her testimony had on others. Praise God! Our faith can also touch the lives of the people around us.

How Can We Know for Sure?

Such people are false apostles, deceitful workers, masquerading as apostles of Christ. And no wonder, for Satan himself masquerades as an angel of light.   —2 Corinthians 11:13-14

Millions of bills and coins trade hands every day. Paper money is usually made from a special blend of linen and cotton. It is nearly impossible to replicate, yet some have created passable reproductions that we call counterfeit. There are many ways to identify counterfeit money, however. At the grocery store, the cashier can swipe bills with a pen that leaves an amber-colored mark if the cash is authentic. If it leaves a black or brown stain on the bill, it fails the test. An ultraviolet light also helps to confirm whether the cash is genuine.

I've sometimes wondered how I would react if the cash I handed to the clerk were counterfeit. First, I'm sure I would be embarrassed. Then I'd probably get angry, thinking that someone had passed it on to me and I would have to absorb the cost. Even worse, I hope I wouldn't be suspected of counterfeiting!

Christ warned about false prophets and teachers that will attempt to influence us before he returns (Matt. 24:24). Simon the sorcerer in Samaria was a false teacher, and he mistakenly thought he could buy the Spirit's power (Acts 8:18-20).There is much more at stake if we are fooled by the lies of false teachers. We must be vigilant, knowing the truth of the gospel.

To prepare ourselves to discern false prophets and teachers, we need to read God's Word, the Bible, each day. It contains all the wisdom we need for living God's way. Most important, the Bible tells us clearly that salvation is available through Jesus Christ alone. Be on guard! Satan himself will sometimes impersonate an angel of light.

Question new ideas and search the Scriptures for agreement. Believe God's promises in the Bible. Pray for discernment and wisdom. The Holy Spirit, living in our hearts, will guide us into all truth (John 16:13).

Reckless Persecutor

Jesus said, ". . . Love your enemies and pray for those who persecute you, that you may be children of your Father in heaven."
—Matthew 5:43-45

The words of the reckless pierce like swords, but the tongue of the wise brings healing. —Proverbs 12:18

Words have the ability to build up or tear down. As family members, friends, and coworkers, we must realize the power we have in the words we speak.

I was at my water aerobics class the other day when I ran into a woman I had worked with when I was in high school. I recognized her immediately, and memories rushed to the surface of the ways she had mistreated me in the small office we worked in. My job was to assist her with the book-keeping. If I made any errors in recording or accounting, she would point it out loudly, to me and everyone else within earshot. It seemed she took joy in making me miserable. I was only 17 years old and had no idea how to handle the situation. Her words hurt and although I kept quiet, I held resentment in my heart. I was thankful when I left that position to head off to college. I had forgotten about that nasty person. But now here she stood before me in the locker room. My stomach tightened.

"Hi. Are you Mary?" I asked without thinking. "Do you remember me? I used to work with you at Wilde's."

"Oh, my," she said, not missing a beat. "You've gotten older and put on some weight."

Wow! She was able, in so few words, to ruin my day. If anything, she had gotten more skilled at putdowns. The temptation to "hit back" was tremendous. I think maybe the Holy Spirit intervened at just the right moment.

"You haven't changed a bit," I shot back. By her reaction, it seemed she took it as a compliment. I managed to be truthful without being hurtful. Now that I'm an adult, I can see that she is an angry and bitter woman, obviously deeply wounded, using an effective defense that lashes out at others and keeps them at a distance. Understanding that makes it easier to ignore her comments.

I am commanded to love Mary. So . . . I will. Though she didn't persecute me for being a Christian, she did mistreat me (and probably many others) in other ways. I will be kind, tolerant, and forgiving, because I know "I can do all this through him who gives me strength" (Phil. 4:13).

God's Not Finished with Me Yet

He who began a good work in you will carry it on to completion until the day of Christ Jesus. —Philippians 1:6

Ananias, a Jewish Christian in Damascus, placed his hands on Saul, professing that Jesus had sent him so that Saul could regain his sight and be filled with the Holy Spirit. The Spirit had already been active in Saul's heart by convicting him of his sin (John 16:8). But now, with the assurance of Ananias's message from God, the healing of his eyes, and the filling of the Spirit, Saul was empowered for service.

When I asked Jesus into my heart as a child, the Holy Spirit began a good work in me. I was made aware of sin; it was revealed to me by the Word and the Holy Spirit. This is a process that is ongoing yet today. I walk closer to my Lord now than I did at the age of nine. I have a desire to grow in knowledge, wisdom, and grace. I am encouraged by Scripture's promises that I can, through the Spirit of Jesus, do that (2 Cor. 3:18).

Do you see growth in your spiritual life? Do you believe the promises in the Bible? If so, God has begun and will continue a good work in you! If not, receive Christ today and invite him to transform your heart, for "everyone who calls on the name of the Lord will be saved" (Acts 2:21).

Lesson 7
S-T-R-E-T-C-H-E-D

Acts 9:32-12:24

We have discovered that in one way and then another the early believers who made up the newly formed church were being stretched in their life of faith. Despite persecution, the gospel was spreading through Jewish communities from Jerusalem to Judea and Samaria and beyond. Next we encounter another stretch that helps to fulfill Jesus' great commission to spread the good news "to the ends of the earth" (Acts 1:8)—to non-Jews, or Gentiles.

Opener (optional)

Name a movement or institution that from the outside seems too big to be changed. Is it really unchangeable? Think of examples in which things seemed to be permanent but for some reason were not. What happened?

EPISODE 1

Acts 9:32-43

1. This next section of Acts focuses on the movements of Peter. Where does he go? How does the Lord work through Peter to show his care for the community of believers?

To think about as you discuss . . .

- what happens in Lydda (see also Luke 5:17-26; Acts 3:6-7; 5:15)
- how news spreads, calling Peter to Joppa
- what happens among the community in Joppa
- Peter's willingness to serve in these situations

Peter's Travels

Acts 8:14-17 reports that "the apostles in Jerusalem . . . sent Peter and John to Samaria." The *NIV Study Bible* explains that "the Jerusalem church assumed the responsibility of inspecting new evangelistic efforts and the communities of believers they produced (see 11:22)." Peter's travels "about the country" (9:32) were likely linked to this purpose, and he worked to encourage and build up the communities he visited.

Acts 10:1-8

2. Who is Cornelius, and what does he learn through a vision? How does he respond?

To think about as you discuss . . .

- Cornelius's role in the army and his nationality
- Cornelius's moral standards and spirituality
- whom he sends to Joppa

Acts 10:9-23a

3. What does Peter learn from the vision he receives?

To think about as you discuss . . .

- why Peter went up to the roof and what was on his mind
- what God tells him about food (compare with Lev. 11; see also box on next page)
- how Peter reacts at first, based on Jewish tradition
- what the Spirit tells Peter about his visitors

4. How does Peter show he has understood the message and is beginning to change his thinking?

To think about as you discuss . . .

- the Spirit's command to Peter
- the visitors' report that an angel had spoken to Cornelius
- Peter's invitation to the visitors (recall Acts 2:46)

Caesarea (ruins pictured above) was located about 30 miles (48 km) up the coast of the Mediterranean Sea from Joppa. It was a busy harbor city and the center of Roman government in Judea (see Acts 23:23-35). Built by Herod the Great and named for Caesar Augustus (see Luke 2:1), it was a showcase of Roman culture.

As a centurion there, Cornelius was a Roman army officer in charge of a hundred soldiers in the Italian Regiment (Acts 10:1). In the Roman military, a regiment consisted of about 600 men, and ten regiments made up a legion (6,000). Regiments were designated by names; another one mentioned in Acts was the Imperial Regiment (27:1).

Clean and Unclean, Jews and Gentiles

For centuries the Jews had been taught, as part of their law, to avoid certain foods so that they, as a people, would be set apart from other nations (see Lev. 11). They were taught that

- **land animals** that had a split hoof and chewed cud, such as cattle, goats, sheep, and deer, were clean. All other land animals, such as camels, lions, pigs, weasels, rats, lizards, and snakes, were unclean.
- **water creatures** that had fins and scales were clean. Others, such as catfish, eels, and shellfish, were unclean.
- **birds of prey and carrion eaters** were unclean. Some examples were eagles, vultures, hawks, ravens, owls, storks, and herons.
- **insects** that flew or walked, except those with jointed legs, were unclean. Locusts, katydids, crickets, and grasshoppers were clean.

This led to a misunderstanding that the people of other nations (Gentiles) were also unclean. Even entering the house of a Gentile or eating with them was thought to be unclean (see Acts 10:28). But that was not the intent of God's law. Now that Christ had come and fulfilled the law (Matt. 5:17-20), foods that were previously unclean were now declared clean, and the Jews were called (again) to welcome believers from all other nations into the kingdom of God. This abrupt change was difficult for many Jewish Christians, and it led to conflicts within the early church. But the Lord now made clear that his people should "not call anything impure that God has made clean" (Acts 10:15). Notice that Jesus even laid the groundwork for this change in his teachings in Matthew 15:10-11 and John 10:14-16.

Acts 10:23b-48

5. How does Peter show and explain his full acceptance of Gentiles (non-Jews) as he meets with them? How does Cornelius show his trust in God and his expectation that God will work?

6. How does God reveal his presence while Peter is speaking? Why is this surprising? How is it affirming?

To think about as you discuss . . .

- the events of Pentecost (Acts 2:1-4)
- the Spirit's outpouring on Gentiles as well as Jews
- how the presence of other Jews gives credibility to this event

7. What does Peter conclude from this? Why? (vv. 47-48)

Acts 11:1-18

8. How does Peter answer to the objections he hears from the leaders in Jerusalem? What do they conclude, and why?

What does this mean to me?

- What does this episode teach us about accepting people into the family of God? What about someone who . . .
  —has a different ethnicity or cultural background?
  —has a different worship style?
  —is in a different income bracket?
  —is different in other ways?

- Is there anything you need to do to be more open to other people and other ways of doing things? Explain.

EPISODE 2

Acts 11:19-24

9. How do the church leaders in Jerusalem respond when they hear about other Gentiles (Greeks) believing in the Lord? How does Barnabas assess the situation?

Acts 11:25-30

10. Describe Barnabas and Saul's activities in Antioch. What were the results? What else happened at this time?

To think about as you discuss . . .

- Barnabas's giftedness and personality (see 4:36-37; 9:26-30)
- the effects of Barnabas and Saul's teaching
- the believers' response to the great need of others

Acts 12:1-24

11. What were Herod's intentions? What did he gain by this? What did he lose?

To think about as you discuss . . .

- what Herod did to the apostle James and why
- why Herod arrested Peter and what happened to Peter
- what Herod did to Peter's guards
- what Herod thought of himself and how God dealt with that

Which Herod?

The King Herod in Acts 12 is Herod Agrippa I, grandson of Herod the Great, who was king of Judea when Jesus was born (Matt. 2). Herod Agrippa's uncle, Herod Antipas, was the ruler who beheaded John the Baptist (Mark 6:14-29) and interrogated and mocked Jesus (Luke 23:6-12). Herod Agrippa II, who succeeded his father, Agrippa I, later heard the good news of Jesus from Paul (Acts 26; see Luke 21:12).

What does this mean to me?

- What does this episode reveal to us about the power and motivations of human leaders and political systems?

- What do we learn here about the power of God and the Word of God?

Explore!

- S-t-r-e-t-c-h yourself. Invite someone over for dinner or out to coffee who is different from you in a significant way. Begin working on a friendship with that person, and aim to make it last. Give thanks to God for the creativity and diversity with which he made humankind.

- Journal about your favorite traditions (holiday, religious, family, other). Explore the origin and significance of each, their connection (if any) to the Bible, and why they are important to you. Are they inclusive or exclusive? Do they cause unity or discord? Ask the Spirit to help you discern what you should cherish in them in the light of God's grace.

- Check out Jewish traditions that are popular today by visiting www.myjewishlearning.com and similar websites. Compare holidays to the Old Testament feasts described in Leviticus 16, 23, 25, and Esther 9. Check out Christian traditions and holidays and their history at www.christianity.about.com and www.religionfacts.com/christianity.

Break Away (at-home readings)

Mistaken Identity

"People look at the outward appearance, but the Lord looks at the heart."
—1 Samuel 16:7

A man in my neighborhood died recently. I had known him for many years. We had visited with him and his sweet wife regularly until she died of a stroke. He was somewhat rude and crude, often making jokes that were actually hurtful. At times he was unnecessarily rough with my children as he played with them, bruising them and making them cry. In my heart, I felt that he was sometimes cruel and thoughtless to his wife.

After her death, we stopped visiting him. I didn't send him Christmas cards or call to make sure he was all right. We no longer stopped in for coffee or invited him over for Sunday dinner. I felt justified in my behavior because he was so difficult to be around, not realizing the sinfulness of my attitude.

When I attended his funeral, tears streamed down my face as I listened to many stories of his kindness and generosity. His son remembered his dad singing praise hymns in the barn as he milked early in the morning.

His granddaughter read a poem she had written for his 80th birthday. A neighbor shared, in a trembling voice and with many tears, how John had knocked on her door one winter day, handing her a check. Her family had been in hardship and had faced humiliating relationship conflicts. She had six children, and that money provided gifts for Christmas that year.

"Oh, Lord," I prayed where I sat, "forgive me for assuming I knew who this man was. Forgive me for not showing him love."

Has someone specific come to mind while reading this? With Christ's strength, you can make the first step of reaching out. God is quick to forgive when we repent of our attitudes and behaviors. Make that phone call, walk across the street, write a letter or email, begin to rebuild a broken relationship. Do so before it's too late and you've missed the opportunity.

Giving Generously

If the willingness is there, the gift is acceptable according to what one has, not according to what one does not have. . . . for God loves a cheerful giver.   —2 Corinthians 8:12; 9:7

My friend, Mary, has lived on a limited income since she was disabled from a car accident. With a monthly income of $757, she sometimes has difficulty deciding which bills to pay. The opportunity of going to college brought more challenges. Most of the education costs were covered, but coming up with enough gas money was nearly impossible. Her faith was strengthened as she often found gift cards for a local gas station in her mailbox. She also took that as confirmation that she was doing as God wanted her to.

After Bible study one Thursday morning, Mary told me that she was struggling with giving. She wanted to give 10 percent back to God (based on the Old Testament tithe—Deut. 14:22-29), but she told me that if she were to put $75 in the offering plate, another bill would go unpaid.

I suggested she pray about this, asking the Spirit for guidance, and consider giving what she knew she could give cheerfully—and then to try building on that as God continued to provide for her. It might take a while, even years, but eventually she might be able to give even more than 10 percent!

Many Christians who excel in giving are able to do far more than that, cheerfully and generously, as God provides.

With the Spirit's wisdom we recognize that everything we have, including our money, belongs to God, and that he calls us to give him our whole life and being (see Luke 20:20-26; 21:1-4; Rom. 12:1-2). So whatever we can give, according to our means, let's give it cheerfully, as Paul suggests to the Gentile Christians in Corinth (2 Cor. 8:8-15; 9:6-15). And let's trust the Lord to continue providing and to guide us so that we can give more and more for his kingdom, to the praise and glory of God the Father.

From Broken to Beautiful

God demonstrates his own love for us in this: While we were still sinners, Christ died for us.   —Romans 5:8

In Joshua 2:1-21 we read of a prostitute named Rahab. She helped Israel gain victory over Jericho. Take a moment to read that passage. Picture Rahab, the flax on the roof, the king's men in search of the spies, Rahab's conversation with the two spies, the scarlet cord hanging from her window.

Rahab made her living as a harlot. I assume she was a wounded woman living in disgrace. But when the Israelite spies came to her door, she was willing to risk her life by hiding them. Hebrews 11:31 says that "by faith the prostitute Rahab, because she welcomed the spies, was not killed with those who were disobedient."

Aside from rescuing her and her family, God heaped blessings on Rahab. In Matthew 1:5 we see that this Gentile woman came into the community of Israel and was even grafted into the genealogy of Christ our Savior.

The record of Rahab demonstrates that our God has amazing love for us. His plan for our lives is nothing short of miraculous. Does this story give you hope in your situation, or for someone you care about? God's love for us overcomes the sins we've committed. His forgiveness can change us from broken to beautiful.

Lavishly Loved

See what great love the Father has lavished on us, that we should be called children of God! And that is what we are!   —1 John 3:1

We've been learning that the good news of Jesus was spreading to Gentiles and that they were becoming "children of God" (John 1:12), "fellow citizens with God's people and also members of his household" (Eph. 2:19).

God has several names that describe his attributes, but did you know that Jesus most often referred to him as "Father"? Sometimes Jesus also called him "Abba," which in the Jewish culture is like our word "Daddy."

I didn't have a great relationship with my earthly father. I share this experience with many women and girls, considering the shelves and shelves of books that deal with abusive, absent, or emotionally distant fathers. That relationship affected my faith walk with my heavenly Father immensely. I couldn't fathom what it would be like to know the love of a father. I had only known harshness, disapproval, and impatience. His touch was never tender or welcome.

When I was introduced to my heavenly Father in Mrs. Frey's fifth-grade Sunday school room, I expected the same harshness, disapproval, and impatience from God. Why would I anticipate anything different? My relationship with God was "safe" and very distant for many years.

I met and married a wonderful Christian man. When we started a family of our own, I caught a glimpse of how a loving father relates to his children. He was tender, and yet firm when they needed it. His patience was never-ending. He enjoyed holding our babies in his arms and playing with them on the floor. He would cuddle them in his lap as he read bedtime stories and prayed with them as he tucked them into bed.

I began to mourn for the little girl that never had the security and love that my children learned to expect. I found myself going through the process of mourning, experiencing anger, denial, and finally the acceptance that my earthly father wasn't able to show me love. Now I'm learning how to be a child of God, to accept his love and grace. He has miraculously met my needs, and I am discovering new depths of love that I couldn't imagine.

If you have longed in your heart for a father's love, I want you to know that you *are* loved by the God of the universe. Reach out your arms to him, as a small child would stretch to be picked up, and the Lover of your soul will not fail you. And if you *have* known the love of a father, give God thanks, and, if it's still possible, say thank-you to your dad.

Caring, Growing Stronger—Together

The eye cannot say to the hand, "I don't need you!"

—1 Corinthians 12:21

Recently I injured the pinky finger on my left hand. I dislocated it while play-wrestling with my granddaughter. I was amazed at how difficult it was to accomplish the smallest tasks with the pain that radiated from that tiny part of my body. Annoying as that was, it made me give special attention to it. I protected it to avoid further injury. Without the occasional reminder that it was still healing, I may have overused it.

That reminds me how we should be in the body of Christ. We are all joined together in Christ with different gifts, purposes, and abilities. When one feels pain, we all ought to feel it. When one is happy, we all should rejoice.

In the same way that I guarded my little finger from injury till it could heal, we need to protect our weak and hurting brothers and sisters. What might that look like, to guard and protect the wounded among us? Bringing in a meal? Sending a check? Simply praying for the individual, offering to study the Word with them, helping to attain guidance and counseling, a loving rebuke, offering encouragement, and so on?

If we, as a body, don't care for our hurting members, who will? We need to be sensitive to one another, listening for ways to tenderly show love and concern.

Equally important is caring for people in the body who may be different from us. What makes them different? Why do we think so? What's it like for them to be a part of this body? What if they are hurting? Have we welcomed them with the love of Christ? How can we show we care?

In the process of caring, we offer good deeds for Christ. They are not the root of our salvation, but they are proof of the Spirit living in us.

Lesson 8
To All Nations

Acts 12:25-15:35

I know of a couple who live on a remote little island in the Upper Peninsula of Michigan. In autumn they travel south to Texas in search of a few months of warmer climate and much-needed rest. What makes their journey noteworthy is how they go about it.

Rather than taking the fastest, busiest route by interstate highways, they stick to side roads as they thread slowly but surely through little towns off the beaten path. They stay overnight in bed and breakfast places instead of hotel chains. They eat in "mom and pop" restaurants in hopes of getting to know the local people and the flavor of each area. Their experiences add lots of highlights to their journey.

In this lesson we trek along with Paul and Barnabas as traveling missionaries. They cross water and land to spread the good news of Jesus in distant towns and cities as the Spirit sends them. . . .

Opener (optional)
What's your idea of a successful adventure?

EPISODE 1

Acts 12:25-13:3
1. In your own words, set the scene as the early believers meet in the church in Antioch.

To think about as you discuss . . .
- Paul and Barnabas's return from Jerusalem (see Acts 11:27-30)
- who led the church at Antioch and how they made decisions
- what the Holy Spirit told them to do, and how they responded

Diversity in Antioch

The diverse character of the early church in Antioch is represented in the leadership mentioned in Acts 13:1.

- **Barnabas**—Jewish, a Levite. He came from the island of Cyprus, so he likely descended from Jews of the Diaspora, who were scattered (dispersed) in past centuries, either as officials in Solomon's vast kingdom (1 Kings 4:21), or by the conquest of Assyria (2 Kings 17), Babylon (2 Kings 25), Greek rulers (Dan. 8:5-13, 21-25), Egypt (Dan. 11), or Rome (Luke 2:1-4). (See also Acts 2:5-11.) Barnabas had been a landowner whose name was Joseph before the apostles began calling him Barnabas ("son of encouragement"—Acts 4:36-37).
- **Simeon**—called Niger (possibly a Gentile from the area of the great Niger River in Africa). *Nigeria* means "Niger area."
- **Lucius**—from Cyrene (North Africa).
- **Manaen**—brought up with Herod Antipas, the tetrarch, possibly as a foster brother or cousin to the ruler who killed John the Baptist and interrogated and mocked Jesus (see Mark 6:14-29; Luke 23:6-12). Manaen was thus a Galilean Gentile descended from royalty.
- **Saul**—Jewish, a Pharisee "descended from Pharisees" (Acts 23:6) and a former persecutor of Christians (Acts 9). Born in Tarsus of Cilicia, he probably descended from Diaspora (scattered) Jews, but he was raised in Jerusalem and educated by Gamaliel (Acts 22:3; see 5:34). Saul's father was likely a Roman citizen, and possibly a Gentile convert to Judaism, for Saul was "born a [Roman] citizen" (22:28). His Greek name was Paul (Acts 9:15).

Acts 13:4-12

Use the map on pages 4-5 to track Barnabas and Saul's first missionary journey (reported in Acts 13-14). With a pencil, draw lines from place to place as you read about their travels in the Scriptures for this lesson.

2. What did Barnabas and Saul do on the first part of their journey, and what did they encounter?

To think about as you discuss . . .

- what they did when they got to Cyprus
- who traveled with them and where they went
- who they met, and how Saul knew what to say and do

Another Sorcerer

Just as Peter encountered spiritual resistance in Samaria from Simon the sorcerer (Acts 8:9-24), so Paul and Barnabas were confronted by a "sorcerer and false prophet named Bar-Jesus" (13:6), which means "son of Jesus." This man was also called Elymas (a Semitic word meaning "sorcerer" or "magician"). In many places where the apostles brought the gospel ("good news"), they found opposition from "the spiritual forces of evil" in "this dark world" (Eph. 6:12). Missionaries today testify about similar struggles. (See also Matt. 16:13-20; Eph. 6:10-20; Rev. 1:9-3:22.)

"Saul, who was also called Paul"

In Acts 13:9 Saul is referred to as Paul for the first time. *Saul* means "asked for, prayed for." *Paul* means "small." *Paul* was Saul's Greek name, probably given when he was born a Roman citizen (see Acts 22:3, 27-28). As a missionary to Gentiles, he likely preferred to use his Greek name (see 1 Cor. 9:22-23), and from here on in, the writer of Acts (Luke) calls him Paul. Some interpreters have claimed that Jesus changed Saul's name to Paul at the time of his conversion, but there is no evidence in the Bible for that assumption.

Acts 13:13-52

Continue tracing the line of Barnabas and Paul's journey on the map.

3. Where did the missionaries go next, and what did they do on the first Sabbath in Pisidian Antioch? How did the people respond?

To think about as you discuss . . .

- what they did on the Sabbath
- how Paul presented the good news (compare with Peter's and Stephen's speeches in Acts 2:14-36; 3:12-26; 7:2-53)
- how Paul said they could be forgiven and justified (13:38-39)

4. What happened on the next Sabbath? Why? (Acts 13:44-52)

To think about as you discuss . . .

- who was there and what was different
- how Paul and Barnabas handled the confrontation
- the method of presentation that Paul explained (13:46; see John 4:21-24; Rom. 1:16)

Shaking the Dust Off

Jesus had taught his disciples to shake the dust off their feet wherever people rejected the good-news message of the kingdom of God (see Luke 9:1-5).

EPISODE 2

Acts 14:1-7

Continue mapping the line of Paul and Barnabas's journey.

5. Note the patterns emerging in Barnabas and Paul's ministry work. In what ways is their visit to Iconium similar to that of Pisidian Antioch? In what ways is it different?

To think about as you discuss . . .

- how the unbelieving Jews made trouble, and whom they involved

Ancient sculpture of Zeus

Acts 14:8-20

Continue mapping the missionaries' journey.

6. Name the surprising events that took place in Lystra.

To think about as you discuss . . .

- what happened to the man lame from birth (see also 3:1-10)
- the misunderstanding that developed
- how Paul and Barnabas tried to clear things up and to explain the good news
- how they were prevented from sharing the gospel there
- the price Paul paid for serving Christ (see 2 Cor. 11:24-33)

Legend of Zeus and Hermes

According to an old legend in Greek mythology, Zeus and Hermes once came to visit in the area of Lystra, but no one recognized them or showed hospitality except an old peasant couple. As punishment, the gods destroyed everyone else in the area. The temple to Zeus outside of Lystra (Acts 14:13) was probably built in response to that legend. Seeing that Paul had done a miraculous healing, the people assumed he and Barnabas were gods, and, apparently in fear of the old legend, aimed to honor them to avoid being destroyed.

Acts 14:21-28

Complete the route of Paul and Barnabas's journey.

7. How did it go for Paul and Barnabas in Derbe? Where did they go after that, and how did they sum up their experiences? What did they do to strengthen the churches wherever they went?

To think about as you discuss . . .
- the courage it must have taken to retrace their path
- what they taught as they continued from town to town
- what they celebrated when they returned to Antioch

Roman theater at Attalia (known as Antalya, Turkey, today)

What does this mean to me?
- What have you learned here about the work of spreading the good news? How can God use you in sharing the news of his kingdom?

EPISODE 3

Acts 15:1-21

8. Explain the controversy that developed, and how the church leaders dealt with it.

To think about as you discuss . . .
- the similarity to conflicts that Paul and Barnabas faced on their trip
- the good reports they shared with everyone
- Peter and James's support and proof from Scripture

James in Acts 15 has been identified as the brother of Jesus. He is also mentioned in Acts 12:17 and Galatians 1:19 and is most likely the author of the book of James. (See also Matt. 13:55.)

Acts 15:22-35

9. What does the council communicate to the Gentiles, and what is their response?

To think about as you discuss . . .

- the four restrictions and how these honor God's law (see Ex. 20)
- that Christ fulfilled the purpose of the Jewish ceremonial laws and they are no longer needed (see Matt. 5:17; Rom. 3:17-5:11; Gal. 3; Heb. 7-10)

10. What is the significance of this episode for the church? What does it mean for us today? What does it mean for you, and how can you share that with others?

Explore!

- Learn more about the mission efforts of the apostles and the early church, as reported in the work of historians like Eusebius of Caesarea (4th century) and the accounts of early church fathers such as Ignatius of Antioch and Polycarp. Search out their stories on the Internet or in libraries. On the Internet, search also "missions of the apostles" and visit www.earlychurch.com.
- Make a list of at least five people in your life who do not know or follow Jesus. Pray for them. Ask the Holy Spirit to reveal his will to you and to open the heart of each of these individuals. Ask the Lord to help you see ways in which you can get to know them better, in line with his will. Ask God for the opportunity not only to share the good news of his love but also to show God's love by inviting these people into relationship and community with the body of believers in your church.

Break Away (at-home readings)

Letting God Work

It is by grace you have been saved, through faith. . . . For we are God's handiwork, created in Christ Jesus to do good works, which God prepared in advance for us to do.   —Ephesians 2:8-10

Our pastor challenged each of us to invite one person to come to church with us. Immediately my neighbor's face came to mind. "Really, Lord?" I asked. I had known Shelley for years; we'd gone through school together. But we had taken very different paths. She and her teenagers had moved into the mobile home across the street from us last summer. She had a boyfriend who'd moved in shortly afterward. Our relationship was limited to an occasional wave to say hi as we passed in our cars.

It was clear to me that God wanted me to invite Shelley, but I was nervous about asking. I prayed about it every time I passed by her house. I asked God for an opportunity to invite her to church. It weighed on my mind every time I left my driveway and glanced into her yard.

Then one day I was taking my grandson for a walk and saw that Shelley was outside. "OK, Lord, it's probably now or never," I thought. I met her with a smile, and we chatted about the weather and odd topics. Then, incredibly, these words tumbled out of her mouth: "Are you still going to that church in town?"

"Yes, would you like to come with me? I could pick you up Sunday morning," I said, bowled over by God's amazing work. While he was preparing me to be obedient and courageous, he was preparing Shelley's heart and drawing her to himself.

We serve a holy, marvelous God! He truly is in control. Do you ever have doubts that God has a plan for your life? Go to him and ask for the strength to trust him. Let him work his way, and then sit back and enjoy the ride.

From All Nations

I looked, and there before me was a great multitude that no
one could count, from every nation, tribe, people and language,
standing before the throne and before the Lamb.   —Revelation 7:9

I attended an Easter worship service while on vacation in Washington, D.C.
Coming from a small town in the Midwest, I was amazed to see the diverse
ethnic groups and cultures represented in the church I visited. Many of
the men and women who worked in their national embassies in town were
dressed in their countries' traditional clothing, some brightly colored with
headdresses and others with long shirts of bright linen. They mingled with
the rest of us, who wore American Easter attire.

The music was comfortingly familiar yet at times exotically foreign. Though
the service was in English, I didn't understand all the words of a gentleman
who prayed with a heavy accent. The varied expressions of worship included dancing, lifting up hands toward heaven, and standing humbly with
head bowed and eyes closed. It was refreshing to witness such diverse
worship and to feel free to worship in my own way, praising God personally
and cooperatively in that setting.

Looking around, I caught a glimpse of what the future church might be like
as we stand before God's throne. My heart was filled with joy and awe. I felt
the presence of our Creator, who made us all precious in his sight.

Needless Worry

Whatever is true, whatever is noble, whatever is right, whatever
is pure, whatever is lovely, whatever is admirable—if anything is
excellent or praiseworthy—think about such things. —Philippians 4:8

Because of finances and children, my husband and I have developed a pattern of taking separate vacations. We take quick getaways for one or two
nights, but we don't like to leave the kids for long periods of time. While I
don't recommend this for every marriage, it has worked well for us.

This spring Roger planned to attend a Bike Week in Florida with his friend
Bob. While Bob is Rog's best friend, he is divorced and sometimes goes
out with women that he meets. I totally trust my husband, but Satan is

devious as he looks for a foothold in our lives. I had to chase away many thoughts and fears as I bid my husband good-bye.

Sometimes, while he was away, a suspicious thought would pass though my mind when I least expected it: "What is he doing? Who is he with?" I would have to push the thoughts from my mind. I purposely changed my thought pattern to focus on something uplifting and true. The author of lies would have been very pleased to shake my confidence in my husband, just as he sometimes shook the confidence of leaders in the early church (when they wondered if they should enforce Jewish ceremonial laws, even though God had shown they no longer applied—Acts 10).

Do you struggle with insecurity and worry? If so, ask God for help in focusing on whatever is true, noble, excellent, or praiseworthy.

Insufficient Funds

In him we have redemption through his blood, the forgiveness of sins, in accordance with the riches of God's grace that he lavished on us.   —Ephesians 1:7-8

My daughter, Amber, was upset and near tears when I told her that her checking account was overdrawn. She had two $35 charges against her account for a couple of small purchases.

"I don't have $70 just sitting around to cover that!" she said in exasperation. She worked hard for her money, cleaning horse barn stalls for seven dollars an hour. Doing the math, I realized she would have to sweat for 10 hours to pay for her blunder. I understood her frustration.

I transferred some funds into her account to cover the fees. As much as it hurt my heart, I told her she would have to reimburse me. I was tempted to bail her out, but how would she learn from her mistakes unless she paid the price for them? I felt I should teach her this tough lesson. But then I had second thoughts.

Christ paid the penalty for my sin, which equals much more than an overdraft fee! I deserve to die in my sin, to suffer for the choices I've made. But

Christ willingly took on my sin as well as the sin of the peoples of all nations. He was forsaken as he hung on the cross in our place.

I let Amber stew over the situation for a couple of days before I told her I would cover the cost. I saw a mixture of emotions pass over her—surprise, relief, gratitude, and finally peace. What joy it gave me to remove the burden she had been carrying. It was perhaps a small taste of what my Lord might feel toward me when I show him gratitude, praise, and honor for blotting out my sin and creating in me a new heart.

To Be Continued . . .

Continue in him, so that when he appears we may be confident and unashamed before him at his coming.   —1 John 2:28

As you wrap up this Bible study, you might be asking yourself, "Now what?" Together we've discovered the pouring out of the Holy Spirit on all believers and the spread of the good news to people of many nations. God has used visions to guide his followers and to introduce new truths. In the book of Acts, Luke describes the challenges the early Christians had to face and how they learned from one another and made agreements.

What does that mean to us in the twenty-first century? Christ has not returned yet. We are waiting for his return, as it's described in Acts 1:11: "This same Jesus, who has been taken from you into heaven, will come back in the same way you have seen him go into heaven."

The good news of Jesus ignited a wildfire that continues to spread today. Have you received him as the Lord of your life? Will you invite the Holy Spirit to fan the flames of faith in you so that others will see Christ in you? My prayer is that God will continue to draw you closer to him, that he will reveal his truths to you through his Word, and that you will follow his leading and glorify him in all you do. God bless you!

The following invitation and prayer tools may be helpful to you in approaching God or in helping someone else do so.

An Invitation

Listen now to what God is saying to you. Maybe you are aware of things in your life that keep you from coming near to God. Maybe you have thought of God as someone who is unsympathetic, angry, and punishing. You may feel as if you don't know how to pray or how to come near to God.

- "But because of his great love for us, God, who is rich in mercy, made us alive with Christ even when we were dead in transgressions—it is by grace you have been saved" (Eph. 2:4-5). Jesus, God's Son, died on the cross to save us from our sins. It doesn't matter where you come from, what you've done in the past, or what your heritage is. God has been watching over you and caring for you, drawing you closer. "You also were included in Christ when you heard the word of truth, the gospel of your salvation" (Eph. 1:13). Do you want to follow Jesus? It's as simple as A-B-C:
- **A**dmit that you have sinned and you need God's forgiveness.
- **B**elieve that God loves you and that Jesus has already paid the price for your sins.
- **C**ommit your life to God, asking the Lord to forgive your sins, nurture you as his child, and fill you with the Holy Spirit.

Prayer of Commitment

Here is a prayer of commitment recognizing Jesus as Savior. If you want to be in a loving relationship with Jesus Christ, pray this prayer. If you have already committed your life to Jesus, use this prayer for renewal and praise.

Dear God, I'm sorry for the wrong and sinful things that I've done. I need your forgiveness. I know I need Jesus as my Savior, and I know you listen to sinners who are truthful to you. Please forgive me and help me to live in a right relationship with you.

Thank you, Jesus, for dying on the cross to pay the price for my sins. Father, please take away the guilt that I feel because of my sin, and bring me into your presence. Thank you, Lord, for loving me and saving me.

Holy Spirit of God, help me to pray, and teach me to live by your Word. Help me to follow you faithfully. Make me more like Jesus each day, and help me to share your love and good news with others everywhere. In Jesus' name, Amen.

Bibliography

Arnold, Clinton E. *Acts. Zondervan Illustrated Bible Backgrounds Commentary*. Grand Rapids, Mich.: Zondervan, 2007.

Barker, Kenneth L., and John R. Kohlenberger III. *Zondervan NIV Bible Commentary.* Grand Rapids, Mich.: Zondervan, 1994.

Brand, Chad Owen, Charles W. Draper, and Archie W. England. *Holman Illustrated Bible Dictionary*. Nashville: Holman Bible, 2003.

Bruce, F. F. *The Book of the Acts*. Grand Rapids, Mich.: Eerdmans, 1988.

Courson, Jon. *Jon Courson's Application Commentary: New Testament*. Nashville: Thomas Nelson, 2003.

Elwell, Walter A., ed. *Baker Encyclopedia of the Bible.* Grand Rapids, Mich.: Baker Book House, 1988.

Evenhouse, Neva, and Carol Veldman Rudie. *Discover Acts. The Early Church*. Grand Rapids, Mich.: CRC Publications, 1998.

Evenhouse, Neva, and Carol Veldman. Rudie. *Discover Acts. The Gentile Connection*. Grand Rapids, Mich.: CRC Publications, 1998.

Girard, Robert C. *The Book of Acts. The Smart Guide to the Bible Series*. Nashville: Thomas Nelson, 2007.

Graham, Billy. *The Holy Spirit: Activating God's Power in Your Life.* Nashville: Thomas Nelson, 2000.

Guthrie, D., and J. A. Motyer, et al., eds. *The New Bible Commentary: Revised.* Grand Rapids, Mich.: Wm. B. Eerdmans, 1970.

Harrison, Everett Falconer. *Interpreting Acts: The Expanding Church*. Grand Rapids, Mich: Zondervan Academic, 1986.

Life Application Study Bible: New International Version. Carol Stream, Ill.: Tyndale, 2007.

West, Maude De Joseph. *Saints in Sandals*. Grand Rapids, Mich.: Baker Book House, 1975.

NIV Study Bible. Grand Rapids, Mich.: Zondervan, 2011.

Evaluation Questionnaire

Infuse Bible Studies — Acts (Part One)

As you complete this study, please fill out this questionnaire to help us evaluate the effectiveness of our materials. Please be candid. Thank you.

1. Was this a home group _____ or a church-based _____ program?
   What church?

2. Was the study used for
   _____ a community evangelism group?
   _____ a community faith-nurture group?
   _____ a church Bible study group?

3. How would you rate the materials?
   Study Guide _____ excellent _____ very good _____ good_____ fair_____ poor
   Leader's Notes on website _____ excellent _____ very good _____ good_____ fair_____ poor

4. What were the strengths?

5. What were the weaknesses?

6. What would you suggest to improve the material?

7. In general, what was the experience of your group?

Your name (optional) _____

Address _____

_____

8. Other comments: